*'Courage is the first of human qualities because it is the quality which guarantees all others.'*

Aristotle

First Published in 2021 by Echo Books

Echo Books is an imprint of Superscript Publishing Pty Ltd, ABN 76 644 812 395

Registered Office: Suite 401, 140 Bourke St, Melbourne, VIC, 3000

www.echobooks.com.au

Creator: Thorne Craig, Author

Title: Nerves of Steel: From Full of Life to Life Support.

ISBN: 978-1-922603-01-2 (soft cover)

A catalogue record for this book is available from the National Library of Australia

Book layout and design by Peter Gamble, Canberra

Set in Garamond Premier Pro Display, 12/17, Bernhardt Mod Bold and Minerva Small Caps .

Cover images:

*Samuel–Family holiday in January 2015 (front and back cover)*

*Samuel's MRI scan 29/11/2015 (front cover)–T2 Weighted Sagittal Spinal Cord (image inverted)*

*Samuel's MRI scan 29/11/2015 (back cover)–T1 Weighted Axial Brain Image Gadolinium Enhanced*

# Nerves of Steel

## From full of life to life support

## A young boy's courageous fight to survive Transverse Myelitis

# Craig Thorne

((( echo )))
BOOKS

# Contents

# Preface

I made a decision in the first weeks of Samuel's hospital admission that not only did I *want* to write a book, I actually *would*. There are paragraphs and sections here that are unchanged from when I first penned them in December 2015, in hospital, while waiting for Samuel to regain consciousness. In the early days, my jottings were a release of pain and emotion that by themselves would barely have made a blog. My beautiful wife, Jane, kept daily notes, which, along with a daily photo record and recollections from our wonderful daughter Amelia, are what allowed the book you are now reading to exist.

Included in these pages are the text messages we sent to family and friends to keep them updated on Samuel's progress. These messages offered a somewhat sanitised account of those weeks and months, because while we wanted to give information, we were also intent on conveying a sense of hope. As 2016 began and the reality of the length of the journey ahead emerged, we realised daily messages were not sustainable, and reduced them to weekly updates. Much of the ugly and difficult detail was omitted, but these brief synopses remain unedited and original to convey the story in a raw yet personal way. They are printed in full in Part 4, with a snippet or two at other relevant places throughout the book, to offer a slightly different perspective on the events I've recounted.

This book is not a blueprint for others to follow, but I hope it may help other families unfortunate enough to find themselves in similar circumstances, to make one for themselves. Every situation will be unique. Read it once, or twice. Ask others to read it too—perhaps they will see something you haven't, or it might be just enough to spark ideas for a solution to what others are facing, or how you could help.

People often say to us that they couldn't do what we have had to do, or endure what we have had to endure, but we know they would be surprised by what they are capable of. This is because, for them, our situation is largely hypothetical—not because they don't want to genuinely engage with the most horrific of concepts and experiences, but because their brains simply won't allow them to fully overlay such a devastating situation upon the context of their own family unit. For those who have gone through complex or debilitating situations themselves, it is real, but hypotheticals can never really test the true strength of human capacity, endurance and love.

Our heartfelt thanks go to all those people who have supported us throughout this difficult journey, including family, friends and volunteers, as well as the many medical and educational professionals, some of whom you will encounter in this book. It is with their support that our capacity to endure has ultimately withstood.

Our only choice was to move forward doing what we could—to do whatever it would take and to never give up.

Craig Thorne

# Foreword

My son Craig asked me to write an Introduction to a story about a series of events that no parent should ever have to confront. This 'out of nowhere' occurrence had the potential to tear his family asunder, despite the love each showed to the other—Craig, Jane and their two children, Amelia and Samuel.

This story is confronting. It is compelling. Unashamedly, Craig reveals all of the raw emotions he experienced in a terrifying roller-coaster ride. I believe Jane suffered all of the same emotions, but perhaps at an even deeper level—she was a mother, a devoted mother.

At the age of nine, Sam went from a healthy, sports-loving, budding musician to a quadriplegic in a matter of hours. Not only a quadriplegic but also requiring a tracheostomy and a ventilator to allow him to breathe. Sam cannot swallow and is fed through a tube directly into his stomach. Thus, he became completely dependent on medical devices to sustain his young life.

Fate had struck a devastating blow. Transverse myelitis. This is a neurological condition few medical practitioners ever see in a lifetime of practice. Craig's idealistic family life had changed for ever—never to return.

I saw Sam a few days into his induced coma. Lifeless body. Tubes everywhere. I railed against such gross injustice, such unfairness. My heart bled for Sam, and his family. How I would have willingly given everything to change places with him. A young life thwarted—his potential restricted? Hopefully not!

The intense emotional pain, the draining of every ounce of mental and physical energy, the innumerable anxious moments, the never-ending trials and tribulations, the not knowing from one minute to the next, all took an immense toll on Jane, Craig and sister, Amelia: not to mention the toll on Sam's emotional and mental wellbeing.

But nothing shook the family's absolute commitment to Sam. His best interests took precedence, nothing else was important. I was there.

This story must be told. Craig has relived the harrowing moments of each of those 480 days to tell his story. It is his fervent hope that this book will be of material assistance to parents facing a serious medical crisis, to their relatives, friends and children—and not least of all, to all medical and allied health professionals. There are lessons to be learned by one and all.

I witnessed the living hell experienced by Samuel, Craig, Jane and Amelia—the experiences gained from their journey cannot, and must not, be wasted.

Eric Thorne

GOVERNMENT HOUSE
QUEENSLAND

## Message from the Governor of Queensland

This account is both harrowing and inspirational: harrowing for Samuel's uninvited calamity and its consequences for him and for his loving family; inspirational for his stoicism and the determination of them all – Craig, Jane, Amelia and Samuel – to achieve the best outcome available.

I applaud Craig for writing this book, which will have taken a lot of courage and persistence – and his wish to help others get through similar challenges.

But the cruel blow dealt Samuel really stands alone. I join with all Queenslanders in wishing his life will be as happy and productive as he and his family and their supporters are determined it will be.

**Paul de Jersey AC CVO**
Governor of Queensland

# Testimonials

'At some stage in your life, your moral courage will be tested by a difficult challenge. How might you react? Will you have the strength to deal with that adversity? Here's an example of how some very special people had to cope with a serious crisis. This powerful book graphically outlines the life-changing challenges faced by Samuel and his family, and how they managed to respond. An inspiring book. Please read it.'

Tony Ryan

Educator, Writer, Futurist

Author of 'The Next Generation'

'*Nerves of Steel* is a story of resilience, as a family journeys from disorientation to reorientation when an unexpected illness upturns their world. The reflective and measured approach taken by Craig Thorne allows those working within a hospital setting to truly see the impact that each decision they make can have when delivering care.'

Shail Maharaj

Senior Paediatric Physiotherapist.

Queensland Paediatric Rehabilitation Service

'*Nerves of Steel* is an absorbing and uplifting must-read for health professionals and anyone involved in providing care for others.

In our lives we may experience pain that feels endless, situations that appear hopeless, or waiting that seems unbearable. This inspirational story reminds us of the importance of being person-centred in how we think and act. It invites us to trust in the power of connection, to never give up hope and to believe that fulfilling your potential is always within reach, even in the face of overwhelming odds. It narrates a lived experience that lifts each of us and invites us to trust in and harness the power of human connection. It is about resilience, about family, about never giving up—and at its heart it is about the power of love. It will inspire you to create something beautiful out of the circumstances that life brings your way.'

Associate Professor Frank Tracey

Chief Executive

Children's Health Queensland Hospital and Health Service

'Samuel is an inspirational, intelligent, kind-hearted and humorous young man and *Nerves of Steel* is the remarkable story of his family and what is achievable through love, advocacy and commitment. With these, Samuel won't just survive, he will thrive. The message for readers is that there is always hope.'

Michelle Bond

Educational Leader

'I only crossed paths with Samuel and his family relatively recently and we have a common bond. A bond shared by more than 20,000 Australians suffering with paralysis.

Those of us who suffer with paralysis and those closest to us know only too well the fear and pain that comes with uncertainty. We know the frustration and hopelessness that comes with serious limitation. We know what despair and loneliness really feels like. Despite these challenges, Samuel is an inspiration to us all. His positive attitude affects everyone around him.

As a community we have the power to decide what is socially important. Now is the time to invest in medical research and new treatments, create new technologies and new industries, and remove the burden of paralysis from innocent men, women and children. Everything is possible!'

Perry Cross–Founder & Executive President

Perry Cross Spinal Research Foundation

C2 Ventilated Quadriplegic

'Samuel is the strongest person I think I have ever met. His courage and resilience leave me in awe—and were an inspiration to me throughout my 2016 Rio Paralympic campaign. But it's his remarkable character strengths— exhibited daily—that have left a lasting impression with me. His strength, determination and resilience are astonishing.

In telling Samuel's story, Craig takes the reader through the ups and downs of surviving transverse myelitis and offers strategies that can help others through life-changing times. Knowing Samuel's story helped me. Reading *Nerves of Steel* can help you, too.'

Matt McShane

Australian Paralympian—Aussie Rollers Basketball Team

'Spinal cord injury has a devastating effect on people and those around them. Craig's work gives us an insight into what the journey is like from a parent's perspective. Nothing tugs more at the heartstrings than to read the words born out of the love for a child. Check it out.'

Dr Dinesh Palipana, OAM, LLB, MD

Queensland doctor and quadriplegic

# Part 1—Samuel's Story

# The Slightest of Sniffles

## Before transverse myelitis

I had taken a few days leave from my job as deputy principal of a large Brisbane state school. It was November 2015. My daughter Amelia was about to graduate from Year 12 and I wanted to make sure I was there to celebrate and savour the moment.

The bonus was spending extra time with my nine-year-old son, Samuel.

Watching him play in an interschool basketball game and seeing his dedication and commitment to his teammates filled me with great pride and happiness. My quiet pride increased when he later confided to me in that 'I'm-telling-you-this-but-don't-really-need-you-to-do-anything' kind of way, about some disappointment he'd felt after the match.

I loved doing the afternoon school runs with Jane. Samuel, in the backseat, would leap forward the instant we stopped to pick up Amelia, ripping up his shirt and blasting the air conditioning from the centre dashboard onto his chest. He had a trick where he could make his stomach muscles ripple in waves—I had no idea how—a feat he was happy to repeat for the kids at his Friday-night swimming club. At nine, he already had his five-year membership award and a host of other swimming medals for most improved and champion at stroke, as well as competition ribbons, overflowing his albums. Extracting him from the water, whether it was the pool, the surf or the shallow flats of

*Amelia & Samuel–September 2015*

our favourite Keppel Sands holiday destination, was often difficult due to his inner piscatorial drive.

He had a growing passion for rugby league, driven in part by lunchtime games with school friends as well as watching the huge on-field hits of his idol, Sam Thaiday. Somehow, he also managed to fit in tennis lessons and was progressing with cello classes to the point where he would confidently try to instruct unteachable-me in the nuances of up strokes, down strokes and finger placement. I had been uncoordinated as a child, so Samuel's athletic prowess was both a surprise and a joy. We would find him in the hall, back pressed nearly to the ceiling after literally climbing the walls. And he was fearless: the noise his 'Green Machine' bicycle made skidding down the same footpath he'd once stacked it on, breaking a tooth, heralded to the world that Samuel was in it—and he was getting ready to take it on.

*On the 'Green Machine'*

In quieter moments he loved reading, a passion he shared with his sister. At bedtimes he would frequently disappear into the toilet to read 'just one more chapter'. Sometime later I would need to force open the door—he would jam a foot against it to try to stop me—and remove the book from his tight little grasp, only to close the door to the sound of laughter as he picked up the next book that he had hidden behind it.

As parents we often like to say we should spend more time with our children. But for the previous year or so, I was no longer paying lip service to this. I had genuinely reflected on how I spent time with the kids—different for both—and had committed to making it real for me, and real for them. Though I couldn't have known it at the time, the hours spent with Samuel mastering the art of boomerang throwing, or practising spiral passes and drop kicks in the front yard, have become cherished memories, and I am grateful for them.

Something that had helped me to focus on 'the now' was the gift of a memory jar, given to our family by close friends at the start of the year. The concept was simple: we would each write brief notes on pieces of paper about family events as they happened throughout the year, fold them and place them (anonymously) into the jar. By the end of the year, it would be full. The idea was that on New Year's Day, we could open them and take turns to read out random notes, laughing and bonding over a year's worth of happy memories.

Throughout 2015 we had each focussed on filling the jar without any thought that we may never want to open it. For now, Samuel was fit and healthy, and had the world at his feet.

## Admission

Several weeks later, it was a Friday night and for once swimming club had taken a back seat to the school disco. Samuel had had the slightest of sniffles earlier in the week, but this was now a distant memory and he was excited about the night ahead. I had been away for a week, leading my school's annual Canberra tour, and so, at Jane's insistence,

*Leaving for the overnight Sea World excursion*

Samuel agreed to let me accompany him to the door. A polite boy, he managed to contain his impatience when there was a brief delay at the entrance over some ticketing confusion, and then he was off—running excitedly to join his mates, eager to relive their experiences of the all-you-can-eat seafood buffet at Sea World, where they had been for an overnight school excursion during the week.

It wasn't a late night, but it had been a busy week and we were all happy to get to our beds.

Samuel woke around 4:00am with a headache, but not wanting to inconvenience us (one of his thoughtful and unselfish traits), he waited until we got up on Saturday morning to ask for some pain relief. Ever the scientist, he remarked to Amelia that he was experiencing some slight neck pain emanating around 'C2 & C3 vertebrae' and he spent a quiet, restful day watching television. I went to bed early, having spent much of the day with my brother-in-law, visiting from Guernsey. I knew the last two weeks of my work year would be busy with graduation ceremonies and excursions, and I needed to spend some time on Sunday preparing.

Sunday morning, Samuel woke us early for some more pain relief. We suspected his headache was due to exhaustion and slight dehydration—he had had a tiring week—and the slight numbness in his right arm we put down to him having slept on it. But his seasonal asthma seemed to be flaring up, too, and he was needing regular Ventolin from early on in the day. After an inconclusive visit from the out-of-hours doctor in the early afternoon, Jane continued to monitor him while spending time with her younger brother who was visiting that day. At the same time, I tried to get on with my schoolwork. Samuel remained listless: he was off his food, and he'd struggled to grasp a cup at lunch time. We tried some massage and encouraged him to float in the pool for a while to ease the discomfort in his back and arm, but it just made him uneasy and uncomfortable.

Later in the afternoon, I sat working at my laptop in the loungeroom where I could see Samuel. Over about 30 minutes, I observed as he moved from sitting, to lying across the recliner armchair, to then pouring his fluid little body face down onto the carpet. While he claimed he was fine and comfortable, the alarm bells had started to ring louder, and we decided it was time to take him to hospital. The phone rang—the after-hours doctor following up on his visit. Hearing our concerns, he too suggested getting Samuel to hospital as soon as possible.

By then, it was nearly 5:30pm. It was grey and drizzling when we arrived at Logan Hospital, just around the corner from our home. I dropped Samuel and Jane at the emergency department entrance and went in search of a car park. By the time I returned, triage staff had already observed Samuel's wobbly and heavily supported gait. Initial concerns were of meningitis, and after a brief assessment he was ushered into 'Acute 1', a room reserved for patients suspected of contagious/communicable diseases.

Different tests and examinations were puzzling, and the doctors decided an MRI and lumbar puncture would be required. The pins and needles and the numbness had spread to all of Samuel's extremities, and seemed to be progressing back in towards his torso. His asthma was worse, and the Ventolin seemed to be helping less and less.

The first canula was inserted at about 5:40pm, just 10 minutes after our arrival, and we could see a hospital stay was on the cards—although we hoped it would be just a few days. The on-call radiologist arrived at about 8:00pm to complete the initial MRI. Samuel spent nearly 90 minutes lying in the machine after it was decided a second MRI 'with contrast', was required. A special dye was injected intravenously to better highlight the aspects of the scan.

Talk began of transferring him to the Lady Cilento Children's Hospital at South Brisbane, with its paediatric neurology unit. Samuel, feeling all his motor control waning, was outwardly stoic, but whispered to Jane, '*Mum, I don't want to be in a wheelchair.*'

And then it was time for the lumbar puncture. Two careful attempts were made to drain out seven vials of cerebrospinal fluid (three more than usual). Lumbar punctures are not done lightly, and they bloody hurt. But not once did Samuel cry during the process—not even when the needle touched a nerve, causing his left leg to spasm violently.

The ED consultant highlighted to us concerning points from the MRI, which revealed spinal cord inflammation and spots on his brain stem. As he talked to us, we were vaguely aware that the other physicians were taking photographs of the computer screens in front of them—this was not something they had ever seen (outside of textbooks), and they knew it was rare. As we later discovered, most doctors won't ever see a case like Samuel's in their careers.

Transverse myelitis was provisionally diagnosed, and preparations were made to transfer him to Lady Cilento.

While we'd waited, Jane and I had already made a list of items to pack for a few nights in hospital and decided that Jane would remain with Samuel overnight while I took care of things at home. I wrote text messages for my principal explaining the situation and indicating that I expected to return to work on Wednesday. In hindsight, I was clinging to the idea that Samuel's illness was all somehow connected to his asthma—after all he was still complaining of breathlessness—and that the situation would be resolved in a day or two. In reality, the trajectory of our lives was being pushed off course, veering sharply and relentlessly out of our control.

After a quick trip home for a suitcase and belongings, I caught up with the ambulance as it drove out of Logan Hospital just on 2:00am. On board were Samuel, Jane and two paramedics. At this point Samuel was deemed stable enough to transport without a doctor.

Finding a spot in the carpark at 2:30am was easy enough. Gaining access to the hospital using the after-hours push-button intercom was trickier for my exhausted, overwhelmed brain, but soon enough I was striding down quiet corridors, suitcase in tow, heading for the emergency department. There, I was ushered through to Acute Bed 36 to join Samuel and Jane.

Over the next four hours, any number of nurses, registrars and consultants appeared in and out of the room making observations and notes, including the on-call neurological registrar at 5:00am. Exhaustion was setting in—we just wanted to get Samuel up to a ward so he could rest and get treatment started for this transverse myelitis thing, so we could all go home sooner.

By 6:30am, Samuel was very breathless, but staff attending to him declined his quiet requests for his inhaler and I couldn't understand why.

They told us, 'We're just going to move him to a bigger room so we can move around the bed a bit.'

Euphemisms can be a good thing sometimes.

Alternatively: 'We're rushing him to the ED Resuscitation Ward, where numerous lifesaving and preparatory procedures are about to be performed simultaneously by multiple doctors and nurses; where you will be provided with chairs to sit and watch your precious son transition from a state of breathless fear to sheer terror and panic; when (if there is room between the medical staff) you will be able to draw near to your son to comfort him, despite the fact you yourselves will be virtually inconsolable with fear and grief—trying to put on as brave a face as possible.'

'We're just going to move him to a bigger room...' was all that needed saying.

Prior to Samuel's 2:00am ambulance ride, the scenario we'd constructed in our minds involved him spending a day or two on a hospital ward being treated for his malady with a few carefully prescribed and administered drugs. By Tuesday night we imagined him sitting up in bed, devouring a repast fit for a famished nine-year-old boy, and released from hospital by Wednesday—perhaps with a few lingering pins and needles. Jane would be a little worse for wear after a few uncomfortable nights spent on the roll-out bed in his room, and I would be panicking that the house wasn't tidy enough for their homecoming. At barbecues, we would regale friends and family with tales of Samuel's bravery and stoicism through this brief ordeal. Wow!

Instead, through the fog of exhaustion and terror, we were listening to the ED team leader telling us: 'I have made the decision to move to the next level of care by placing Samuel on a ventilator.'

She spoke firmly, with an innate authority that seemed to assert the need for us to trust her and the team. And just like that, we were snapped out of the fantasy scenario we'd been clinging to—into a reality where Samuel's condition was rapidly deteriorating, careening out of control.

A pressure mask had been placed over Samuel's face prior to intubation. I dimly recall someone at the bedside saying they couldn't get a perfect seal, but even so, the mask had the effect of forcing his lips inward over his teeth—a contorted grimace that made it look like he was sobbing with uncontrolled grief. It's a picture I will carry with me to my death. Shocked into action, I buried in, like a second-row forward through the scrummage of medicos, who, by now, had done what needed to be done. I knelt at the bedside, and with Jane by Samuel's head, we tried to convince him he would be okay. My face and tears mocked my words—I have never felt such pain and helplessness before.

We knew he was trusting us and had faith in those around him, but he was terrified, and there was nothing else we could do.

There were doctors and nurses from the ED, from the Paediatric Intensive Care Unit (PICU) and from where else I have no idea—but there were many of them. Porters in red-checked shirts hovered in the background. A social worker had already moved our belongings—

including our optimistically small suitcase—and was encouraging me to follow her upstairs as there would only be room in the elevator for Samuel, Jane and the medical staff. I insisted on staying with him until the last moment. Preparations done, bed loaded with all the necessities for transport, the signal was given and Samuel's journey to the fourth-floor PICU began.

I must have teleported upstairs—I certainly have no recollection of using the elevator—but once there the social worker guided me into a small meeting room. She followed, attempting to make supportive, consoling conversation but I intervened to steal the room for myself, just for a moment. The door closed and my sobbing began. Throughout the preceding hours, I'd mostly succeeded in holding myself together, but the realisation that our lives were about to change, and that Samuel needed us like never before, was overwhelming. My tears were a necessary release but a hopelessly inadequate expression of my emotions.

By 10:00am, Samuel was fully sedated in an induced coma, and on life support. Medications had been administered to relieve his pain, so his stressed and exhausted little body could sleep.

Someone ushered us into the small family meeting room and then proceeded to brief us on Samuel's status. The meeting was a blur, but I think this was when we were told about the steroid treatment that would begin reducing Samuel's spinal cord inflammation—and that we should brace ourselves for a stay in PICU that would number in the weeks (not days), followed by months and months on the wards for rehab. The doctor who had intubated Samuel warned us, 'This is going to be a marathon not a sprint.' While the provisional diagnosis of transverse myelitis had been made, doctors explained the treatment regime would cover a number of neurological possibilities.

By now we were beyond exhausted. The showers we had in the fifth-floor Ronald McDonald House parent rooms were a small relief. They gave us a moment to take stock of the situation, start making phone calls, and pause to just look upon each other's drawn faces, and hug.

## Contact

'I'll come down,' were her Mum's first words when Jane broke the news. By this time, we were composed enough to realise that Jane's elderly mother and sister coming down from the Sunshine Coast would be difficult for them. And while their presence may have provided comfort, it would have served no practical purpose at that time, given the amount of care Samuel was receiving in PICU. As with the voice messages I'd already left for my Mum, and the call I'd made to my Dad from the meeting room earlier, these first phone calls were more about breaking the news and preparing them for updates to follow. Our call to Amelia was the hardest.

In the family tearoom outside the secure doors of PICU, Jane and I discussed how best to tell her the state of play. She had been collected from the Logan Hospital at about 11:30pm the previous evening by her 'bestie', Emma, and Emma's mum. Should we wait to tell her face-to-face, knowing how stressful it might be for her to find her way into the city with Emma? Should we tell her over the phone, knowing that only Emma was with her? Would Amelia cope with the news? How would Emma cope with Amelia getting the news?

In the end, we opted to trust in Amelia's maturity, knowing that she was an intelligent, balanced young woman who had seen her fair share of issues in her seventeen-plus years. We also knew she would cope less well if we were not honest and open with her about the situation.

The exact details of the conversation are lost in the fog of that day, but we began by ensuring Emma was in the house. Support person present? Tick.

Via speaker phone, we explained the situation was not good and tried to tell her what information we knew.

Our faith in her was well rewarded.

Although obviously upset, her first response was practical, measured and entirely focussed on concerns for her brother. She took on board what we were saying, and her calm, clear voice as she started working with us through the immediate implications made it so much easier for us to talk relatively calmly, without 'dropping our bundle'.

After hanging up, she briefed Emma and after figuring out the details of transport to the hospital, the two girls quickly made their way to Samuel's bedside: PICU Bed 36. Finally, our family was together again as we absorbed the reality of what we later found would define our new 'normal'.

Early in the afternoon, Jane and I were able to snatch two much-needed hours of rest in the parents' rooms on level five. Waking at four, we started the next round of texts and phone calls from the family room just outside PICU. This would become a temporary base from which we would make phone calls, greet visitors and make cups of tea. There really wasn't space for such activities in the room where Samuel lay, and we were PICU novices at this point, anxious about intruding or interfering with the goings-on of an intensivist unit—and frankly terrified about accidentally bumping any of the equipment, cords and cables that were keeping our child alive.

At some point, we decided to send our first group text message to family and close friends:

30.11.15–Day 1

> Hi guys some worrying news to share. Samuel is very unwell and been admitted to Lady Cilento hospital where he will remain for a number of weeks... a month... months maybe. Diagnosis is Transverse Myelitis which has affected his ability to use his arms, control his neck, breathe on his own and more... His immune system is attacking the nerve cells. Has been put into an induced coma. Talk soon, thoughts and prayers appreciated. Love Thornes

Samuel was in a coma. Exhaustion, even with a second wind from our afternoon nap, was fast catching up with us. We needed to prepare for the next day (and the next), so we made the difficult decision that it was time to go home to rest. I whispered into Samuel's ear that we were going to do *whatever* it took to get him home and that we were *never, ever* going to give up.

So began the biggest roller-coaster ride of our lives.

# Coping & Hoping

## The Second Day

Samuel seemed more or less the same as we had left him the night before. He looked almost serene, although the myriad tubes and lines going into his body were a stark reminder of the destruction occurring inside of it.

The doctors had explained that transverse myelitis was a neurological condition affecting sections of the spinal cord. We would later learn that Samuel's case was severe and affected most of his spinal cord and parts of his brain stem. It was likely that in developing the antibodies to fight off the sniffle he'd had the week before, his immune system had also created antibodies that were perceiving his own spinal tissue to be a threat to his survival. His own immune system was wreaking havoc on his nervous system and needed to be stopped. At the time, we had no idea how bad the damage would be.

Quarter-inch-wide white ribbon secured the breathing tube going into his throat, pulling slightly against the corner of his mouth. Up close, his eyes were unfocused beneath partially open lids, and dark smudges under his eyes told the tale of the lack of sleep he had endured. A feeding tube snaked across his cheek and disappeared into his left nostril. Multiple intravenous and other lines pierced his skin and a urine bag hung at the foot of the bed, fed by the in-dwelling catheter.

There was no particular smell of disinfectant in the room, aside from the slight scent of the alcohol foam hand sanitiser that was everywhere in the ward. Even so, it felt intensely clean. Two large, heavy-looking horizontal metal arms were suspended from the ceiling. These could pivot independently and from the end of each hung enormous pendants. These were used to support and manoeuvre all manner of equipment: power sockets, oxygen and compressed air, suction canisters and IV pumps, even a nurse's workstation with computers and trays of tools. In Samuel's case it supported the huge ventilator and humidifier providing his lifesaving breaths. ECG sensors stuck to his chest fed constant data to the monitors that were watched by a nurse stationed there twenty-four hours a day.

The nurses gave off an aura of calm reassurance. They were seemingly unfazed by the complexities of the machinery, and measured in their responses to the bewildering array of alarms and other noises. There were long beeps, short beeps, persistent dings, soft pings and the ever-present whoosh of the ventilator, pushing air into Samuel's lungs—not too hard and not too soft—about eighteen times a minute. While we couldn't distinguish the difference in importance of a soft ping or a loud beep, we quickly realised the more critical sounds emanated from the equipment closer to the nurse. But if these were the important ones, how could staff just let their relentless cacophony continue without silencing them and making some intervention for Samuel? Of course, staff were used to these noises—they were trained— but our hearts beat a little faster with each alarm that wasn't immediately tended to. It was classical conditioning in action: each seemingly unattended sound just reinforced our fear, our despair, and our complete helplessness.

During the early days, to compensate for this sense of powerlessness, we would carry out any small task we could that felt helpful. While Samuel was still sedated, we took turns to read to him and wash him as best we could, carefully avoiding the tubes, monitors and drips. Later, we fetched linen or ice to cool him down if he felt he was overheating.

The line between sleep and sedation was not clear. It was difficult to pinpoint the exact moment at which Samuel was brought out of his induced coma, but after a few days, he was fully conscious, although unable to talk. The endotracheal tube passing through his mouth and into his airways was changed after a few days to a nasotracheal tube, which as the name suggests, accessed his airways via his nose. Both of these life-support tubes passed between Samuel's vocal cords, making speech impossible.

After a bit of experimenting, we settled on a rudimentary communication system of blinks: A tight squeeze of his eyes for 'No', rapid blinking for 'Yes'. All we needed to do was control the barrage of questions, often open-ended and simultaneous, from the stream of people coming through the room. I felt increasingly frustrated when it seemed blindingly obvious that a communication process needed to be established, but there was no single staff member who seemed to be taking this on. This was our first indication that we would need to position ourselves as strong advocates for Samuel's needs as the complexities of the support teams increased.

We needed to slow down the bursts of dialogue from health staff, especially once the communications boards were introduced. With these held in Samuel's line of sight, we would point to the letters, words and symbols on the boards and wait for his blinked response. This worked quite well but it was very labour-intensive, requiring one of us to be with him interpreting his conversations. The sheer number of clinicians from different disciplines needing to brief us meant they often wouldn't wait until the parent acting as Samuel's 'interpreter' could join them. They would instead try to talk separately with either Jane or myself. It fulfilled their need to convey important information, but it meant Jane and I needed to spend time later comparing notes. As a mode of communication, it was not sustainable, so we resolved to stick together when conversations were held—staff would need to fit us in to their schedules to deliver their messages. It also meant that both Jane and I could enjoy the early message board conversations with Samuel—moments to be cherished after the traumas of the preceding days. These conversations were frequent during the first critical days and weeks as Samuel's treatment progressed.

There were multiple physio sessions each day to clear his lungs of secretions, attempting to stave off the recurring bouts of pneumonia and collapsed lungs that set back his recovery. While these sessions were critically important, they were difficult to watch: the sight of Samuel's chest being pummelled while tears flowed from his eyes would upset me to the point that I would sometimes need to leave the room, sobbing under my breath. I would have given anything to be on that bed in his place.

A general anaesthetic was required to insert a vascular catheter ('vascath') into his right femoral artery in preparation for plasmapheresis. This treatment, repeated frequently in those first days, is similar to renal dialysis, an attempt to 'wash' his errant immune system of rogue white blood cells with the aim of reducing the severity of the attack on his spinal nerve cells. This treatment was coupled with IVIg—intravenous immunoglobulin— a transfusion process to replace white blood cells with others that would not attack his spinal cord. Only time would tell how successful these treatments might be.

## So Much Going On

On Day 17 of his admission, Samuel underwent a tracheotomy, a surgical incision just below the larynx resulting in a hole called a tracheostomy. This allowed the ventilation circuits to enter directly into his trachea through a curved piece of plastic tubing called a tracheostomy tube or trache (pronounced 'trackie'). At the time, it seemed a drastic solution for a situation we were hoping was only temporary, but it did at least allow him some speech.

We also had a room change to a windowless, awkward space, without a working television for Samuel to watch, but with a different ventilator. The consultants anticipated that as he recovered, Samuel's body would gradually begin to trigger contractions of his diaphragm. Ultimately, he would not need the ventilator, but for now the new machine's screen displayed Samuel's breath volumes and rates, much like the heart rate monitors you might see on a television medical drama. This magic line would change colour to red when it looked like a breath was being triggered by the patient. We saw enough red to buoy our hopes and we shared the news with family and friends:

18.12.15–Day 19

> Day 19 Samuel happy Craig got some av working in tv. Room change to 23. Physio had him pedalling legs on machine with his legs in slings. Machine doing all the work. Samuel used his big toe to tap drum in session with music therapist. Tracheostomy site sore and still getting used to it …. as expected. Most amazing today… was seeing machine show that Samuel has triggered some breaths for about 2 hours. That's a great start. Hopefully he will do this again tomorrow, if only for a short time. Prayers are clearly being answered, thank you! XO :)

But the following day saw no more breaths triggered and that weekend was one of the most depressing we endured. Hopes seemed dashed, and we later learned that a muscle that Samuel could activate between his neck and collarbone was deceiving the machine into thinking his diaphragm was taking over. Thankfully, a couple of senior staff facilitated our transfer to Bed 3—a larger room with windows and space for us to spread out. Bed 3 would be our home-away-from-home for quite some time.

Having a larger room also meant more people could fit into it. About a week after Samuel's tracheostomy, the sutures holding the first trache tube in place against his throat needed snipping by an ENT registrar. Early advice was that this would occur in the afternoon. That morning, the rehab physio team were setting up for a cycling session, so we figured we could let Samuel know a bit later about the planned ENT visit—still giving him plenty of time to get into the right headspace for the procedure. By now, we realised that a bit of warning about planned procedures allowed Samuel to cope better with everything happening around him, and to him.

Suddenly, the ENT registrar waltzed into the room, and with curt disregard for the rehab team, the nurse in charge, and the patient himself, he began preparing to finalise the trache review. The physiotherapist's respectful protests were ignored; it was two days before Christmas and the registrar was obviously on a tight schedule to finish his patient lists.

Fortunately, it was just a simple process to snip two sutures and check the tracheotomy site, but not having the procedure explained ahead of time left Samuel and us distressed. The doctor's lack of any appropriate bedside manner served only to galvanise my resolve to avoid this level of disempowerment in the future.

We had already taken measures to forbid anyone discussing Samuel's potential (or otherwise) for spontaneous breathing—and more specifically, the possibility of 'home ventilation'—within his earshot. A sign on his room door reinforced this direction. It pre-dated our bad weekend of (not) triggering breaths and stemmed from an unexpected conversation with a respiratory consultant that had taken place as we left the PICU one evening. Drawing us aside with his registrar, the consultant had introduced himself and (most respectfully) initiated a conversation about patients who are required to be ventilated in the home environment. The timing was awful. Samuel's case may have been a routine referral for him, but the conversation was pursued without any apparent thought or consideration for where we, as the family, were at in terms of conclusiveness of prognosis and hope. We believed the consultant had been poorly briefed in this instance, and to this day, we have the utmost respect for him. Unfortunately, the hit to our emotional bank account at the time was enormous.

In hindsight, perhaps such unintentional lapses served a purpose as they helped to desensitise us—preparing us for the really bad news that was still to come.

As the days went on, Samuel endured procedure after procedure, many of them painful. The hospital had recently begun trialling a new initiative for its young patients involving 'Bravery Beads', to be given out as a token representing each procedure they underwent during long-term treatment. If the scheme had been fully up and running, Samuel could have made a mile-long string of beads from the hundreds that would have been awarded to him.

Among the treatments was a torturous blood-thinning regime requiring the subcutaneous injection of Clexane (an anti-clotting drug)

into a different site each day. The torture lay not just in the twice daily awful
sting of a needle in either the lower abdomen or upper thighs, it was in how
the injection site was determined. Not to ask him for input about where he
wanted each needle would have been to disempower and exclude Samuel,
but it was a terrible choice to ask him to make. He was forced to accept a
level of responsibility for the pain he was being asked to endure. Mostly, he
opted for his thighs. It was slightly less painful.

Samuel's ability to endure the daily pain and discomfort of his treatment
was a constant source of wonder. He took everything in his stride, often
without whimper or comment, even the neurologist's remark—following the
week six MRI and lumbar puncture—that 'Samuel's transverse myelitis was
not following the typical pathway.' It was a passing remark, but by this time I
had done some research of my own. The floppiness of Samuel's limbs, and the
longitudinal nature of his spinal cord injury, had made me question whether a
diagnosis of acute flaccid myelitis (a somewhat different condition) may have
been more likely. Ultimately, though, the name was unimportant. Whatever
label you put on it couldn't change the situation he was in.

Despite this, Samuel later summed it up neatly in a comment to Amelia
on Day 48, revealing the extraordinary strength of his nine-year-old's
resolve: *It's happened. It sucks that it's happened, but it has. There's nothing we
can do about it. We just need to move on, move forward.'*

## A Raspy Christmas and News Without Cheer

Subtle differences in ventilator settings never went unnoticed by
Samuel. Even if two different ventilators had identical settings, he could
feel minute differences. While other as yet unknown physiological factors
were at play, it was beautiful to hear Samuel's voice—however raspy and
rattly—wishing us a happy Christmas Eve as we arrived that morning. For
the first time since his admission to the emergency department some 25
days before, a small volume of air was escaping past an uncuffed trache tube
and through his larynx. ('Cuffed' traches have an inflatable sac surrounding
them that forms a seal between the tubing and the inside of the tracheal wall.

With no air able to escape past the trache and through his voice box, no speech was possible.) Samuel was determined to make good use of this early Christmas present and spent a good portion of the day gleefully addressing all who entered his room as 'Peasants!'—even Grandma!

A decision had also been made to trial a more portable ventilator at the same time, and this unfortunately made for a pretty ordinary Christmas Day.

If the settings could have been adjusted to support his needs with the uncuffed trache, it would have made for a nice Christmas gift. Instead, Samuel was increasingly uncomfortable with how the new ventilator felt, and as we prepared to make our first social foray—joining two other long-term families on PICU's large balcony—things took a turn for the worse. For the rest of the day, he needed the support of the decidedly unportable bedside ventilator. Jane's mum and sister joined us for lunch in his room at a table that had been hastily set up and decorated.

The one real gift we took from the day was an understanding that we needed to advocate more forcefully for a step-by-step approach to Samuel's health support. Too much had happened too quickly, with decisions and input by too many people.

The motivations for changing to an uncuffed trache and trialling the new ventilator were authentic and well-intentioned: They would allow Samuel to speak and liberate him from his hospital bed—two outcomes that would have been very welcome at Christmas. But Samuel's body had yet to reveal other secrets, and moving too quickly cost him another (double) lung collapse, a bout of pneumonia and an unscheduled (cuffed) trache change on Boxing Day.

I defy any loving and compassionate parent to be able to pick the right moment to tell their child—fit, healthy and active before their illness struck—that for the rest of their life they could be on a ventilator, unable to move their arms and with other motor disabilities. Hope has never, should never, and will never, leave us. But we were also coming to realise that our preparations for the long journey ahead would only be impeded by continuing to deny the ugly, possible truth.

But how to have this conversation? And when?

Sometimes the best moments pick themselves.

*'Mum, when it's time to go home, if my arms are better and my legs haven't improved, will I be able to use crutches?'*

Jane was already at the bedside, wrapping up a session with the speech pathologist, while I was sitting near the windows. She looked at me, then began answering him as the therapist and I exchanged looks indicating that now would be a great time for the session to conclude. The day nurse made herself discretely invisible as Jane and I sat beside Samuel, naming an 'elephant in the room' that needed naming.

Being told that some level of disability was inevitable is something no nine-year-old should ever need to hear. But now was the time.

We spoke about his neurological pathways; his receptive senses travelling to his brain were fairly good, but the motor pathways controlling movement were not. We explained the four differently affected nerves as they had been explained to us: Those that had not been affected; those that were affected and were repairing; those that were affected where it was unknown if they would repair; and those that were damaged beyond repair. There would be some deficit around the spinal cord pathways at C2/C3 level affecting breathing and arms, but we didn't yet know exactly what the extent of this deficit would be.

Samuel seemed to accept that the way his body functioned would not be the same, while also remaining hopefully optimistic for more recovery. He was still the loving, caring and considerate boy he always had been. At the end of our talk, we reaffirmed our love for him and that we were never going to give up.

As brave and stoic as Samuel has been throughout his ordeal, delivering this news broke all our hearts. We hugged (as best we could) and cried together—a single tear from each of his eyes evidence of his internal anguish.

It was the morning of Day 68.

News that Samuel had been given this confronting information spread quickly among the medical practitioners and therapists, with all of them in due course acknowledging the trauma of this cruel milestone. He spoke little of it in the days following. I suspect he shelved the information so he could return to it as and when he wanted. Our social worker made plans for a child psychologist to become involved. Our worry was that Samuel was internalising difficult information without asking any of the questions that might help him clarify and process his feelings; that he would over-prognosticate to the point of complete negativity, despair or despondency. Perhaps a psychologist could weave some magic; to really connect with an intelligent, deep-thinking boy who has always been guarded with his emotional revelations and displays.

I've lost count of the times I've been told that the way children process and deal with trauma can be very different from the way adults do—that they are somehow more resilient. I have always considered myself to be pretty resilient, but the relentless emotional demands of our daily situation had chipped away at my mental strength. How much more difficult must it be for a child, still so hopeful and expectant of significant or full recovery, but who is bound to the physical support of mechanical ventilation and human interventions, simply to live each day, let alone to improve?

Gradually, it dawned on us just how important it was to ensure that Samuel's understanding of the Day 68 conversation was the same as ours. So many times in the first nine weeks, we had uncovered instances where the assumptions and presumptions made by the people around Samuel, did not match *his* understanding. Goodness only knows how often we'd made mistaken assumptions in day-to-day parenting, even prior to his illness.

For example: In his first days in hospital, Samuel had fought hard to prevent his bowels from opening. Why? Careful questioning revealed that he thought he would soil the sheets—no one had explained that his 'special pants' (a better term than 'nappy') would do the trick.

A little later, he had become increasingly distressed about the prospect of his first trache change, worried that he would not be adequately ventilated while it occurred. Until that point, changes to his breathing tubes had been performed under a general anaesthetic. To ensure continuity of respiration, the critical moments of the procedure would take fewer than five seconds, but this had not been made clear when the procedure was first explained. Naturally, he was concerned.

No—not only did we need to clarify his understanding of his prognosis, we had to make clear the likely length of his hospital stay. We hoped a psychologist could help.

# The Three-Month Elephant

## Were Hope to be Set Aside

Day 99 was a Monday. We had noticed a pattern to the weekly activity on PICU: Consultants would return to work after the weekend, consider various observations and reports, then announce the latest adjustments to be made to Samuel's care and management.

Of late, most of these proclamations seemed to emanate from the respiratory department.

Having waited for us to complete a tilt table session—the physiotherapist was short of assistants and needed us to hoist Samuel back to bed—the respiratory consultant requested we join her in a vacant interview room.

As usual, she was succinct and to-the-point. X-rays had revealed that the lower left lobe of Samuel's lungs had not fully recruited (inflated) following his Christmas Day lung collapse. Ventilator pressure settings would need to be reviewed and monitored to remedy this, and that meant Samuel's trache cuff would need to be fully inflated, not just at night, but also during the day. Too much leakage of air around the cuff was making it impossible to maintain the airway pressures needed to reinflate the collapsed area of his lung. While it was a logical intervention, it meant Samuel would again be rendered mute—returning us to the frustrations of the weeks when communication was via alphabet boards, facial gestures and lip reading.

The consultant was at pains to explain the risks associated with long-term lung collapse—mainly, that scarring can render them useless—and this led us to ask: 'Are you telling us that Samuel will be on long-term ventilation?'

It was an awkward moment. The consultant paused, seeming to grapple with a dilemma. Should she share what she knew right now? Or delay answering until the regular weekly family meeting, which included consultants from other treating disciplines? Perhaps, could the question even be referred to the neurology team, which was ultimately overseeing Samuel's case?

No. The answer would come now. It needed to come now.

It seemed, the respiratory and neurology teams had been talking—and we later wondered at what point that conversation was to have been shared with us. Since the beginning of Samuel's treatment, they had pointed to the three-month mark being the likely peak of improvement. It was a milestone I had read about as far back as week one while conducting my own frantic internet searches, trying to find out more about Samuel's diagnosis. I had read, and tried hard not to dwell on, the statistics: roughly one-third of people afflicted by transverse myelitis make a near to full recovery, while another third make a partial recovery with some level of ongoing deficit. The last one-third of patients make limited, if any, recovery.

Calmly and deliberately, the consultant continued: 'While nobody wants to be setting all hope aside, it is looking like Samuel will be ventilated for the rest of his life.'

'While nobody wants to be setting all hopes aside...'

Could this conversation get any worse?

She went on: 'The concern for all ventilator dependent patients is that lung collapses can lead to scarring—bronchiectasis—which renders affected portions of the lungs permanently ineffectual.'

The information reaffirmed our resolve to support whatever it took to recruit Samuel's lower left lobe. But darker questions were now swirling through our minds. Could this bronchi-whatever-it-was spearhead a downward spiral of lung capacity over time? If so, what was the likely life expectancy of ventilated patients?

'We talk in terms of decades. It could be as short as five years, depending on management, and there have been patients who have gone on a lot longer. Look at Christopher Reeve—he went for about twenty years.'

As a comparison, it wasn't as comforting as the consultant may have intended. In any case, as we later discovered, the Superman star survived less than a decade after the horse-riding accident that left him paralysed and on a ventilator.

Picture your own children and do the maths. Do your own maths.

Imagining this possible timeline for Samuel's future was unbearable. Easier to take on board was the vital importance of 'recruiting' his lungs.

Son, your cuff is going up, and staying up, until the respiratory consultants say otherwise! We're getting that left lower lobe up now. While we struggled to process the grotesque enormity of this new information, our immediate priority became full lung recruitment—a good distraction from the developing complexity of the future that now lay before us.

I've never experienced a cricket bat to the back of the head, but I can confidently say this felt worse. Back in Samuel's room, we were stunned and dazed but needing to carry on 'as usual'. The day nurse immediately picked up that something was wrong and had a discreet word with the team leader. Jane overheard them say there was 'nothing in the notes, I'll go and see what I can find out.' It confirmed to us that this latest revelation had not been planned, otherwise the notes may have said: 'Brace for impact; parents about to be totally bewildered, confused, angry, pissed-off, bereft, and in need of timely and caring support.' The nursing staff are great and that day they didn't need notes to know how best to support us. Their calm, instinctive response—to 'give these guys space, watch, and be ready to catch them in a split-second'— was appreciated, even in our misty-eyed, sodden-hearted state.

But it was difficult even to look Samuel in the eyes.

Somehow, we made it to the end of the day. We praised Samuel's efforts in making it to 45 degrees on the tilt table during his physio session, as well as for other therapy milestones. We left him in the care of the night-shift staff with our usual good-byes and routines and headed home.

Neither of us wanted to face our darkest thoughts. Nor did we need or want to talk more about it. We understood the message, and we knew we needed to carry on. We just didn't yet know how.

After a restless night, I was up early, escaping outside for a walk. Setting off into the showery dawn, I was soon outside the Logan Hospital emergency department, wrestling with my fears. I could feel a tsunami of grief building and the first wave of sobbing took hold as I leaned against a pillar outside. I walked on, through the main foyer of the hospital, not far from the room where Samuel had his first MRI. Back outside, the rain was heavier, but at least it masked the tears that were still falling.

I turned towards Riverdale Park, the destination for so many father-and-son outings. As I walked the familiar route that Samuel and I had so often cycled, memories rolled relentlessly into my mind: there was the place where we had practised our boomerang-throwing; there was the fitness trail that Samuel had played on; the open field where we'd kicked a football. Emotions raged through me as I sat on a railing in the rain, wracked by sobs of grief.

Leaving Riverdale, I headed west. The showers had eased and the sun competed with the clouds at my back. I paused for a moment to consider the arc of a rainbow that had appeared in the sky, looking for all the world as if one end of it was coming down in the vicinity of our house.

It was a brief moment of peace and beauty, but as I resumed walking, the rainbow moved (as rainbows do), away from my home. I felt like it was taunting me, reminding me of the pain, grief and loss in my heart.

Giving up has never been an option. But rightly or wrongly, I could not help but think of all that Samuel would *not* be able to do when he finally came home from hospital. Passing the basketball hoop in the small park near our home, I remembered the time, not so long ago, when the four of us had spent a happy afternoon playing there. We'd laughed and attempted crazy shots until we were exhausted. Happy together.

I squatted on my haunches, the rumble of the nearby motorway helping to drown out one final wave of anguished wailing. All my hopes were under siege. I did not care who heard or who saw me. I wanted the world to know I was angry. But I was alone—nobody saw, nobody heard.

That Jane and I had been made the custodians of such definitive bad news was a burden almost too heavy to bear. For Samuel's sake it was critical for us to remain upbeat, positive and supportive, but as we packed the car ahead of our drive to the hospital that morning, Jane and I confessed to each other our reluctance to face the day ahead—Day 100.

It was a low point. Whatever strength we had left was gone, and I believe that it was only by drawing on our marital commitment to one another that we were able to just keep going. We headed into the hospital and, despite our morning 'wobble', just got on with it.

Samuel's program for the day was full. After the regular chest physio, he enjoyed a visit from one of the hospital's therapy dogs, Dexter, a beautiful West Highland Terrier. Then it was time for upper-limb ranging, a therapy that Samuel sometimes found irritating, due to nerve pain and immobility issues.

After that, he was hoisted into his chair for a session with the 'speechies'—our speech therapists. They tempted him with thickened apple juice, dyed an uninviting shade of blue. It was part of ongoing investigations to determine whether he could swallow effectively without liquid entering his airways. I'd had no idea that a speech therapist's role was about more than just articulation of speech. In Samuel's case, it was also about the functioning and integrity of his upper airways, and his speechies were dedicated to making sure his safety was not compromised.

He used the cough assist ventilator (a machine which, as the name suggests, helps patients who are unable to cough, clear secretions from their lungs), and this was followed by a tilt table session where he had some unexpected difficulty in extending his left leg.

At least the 'busyness' of the day made it easier for Jane and me to push the negative thoughts aside and carry on as normal.

Samuel worked (as always) damned hard and by the afternoon he was ready for a well-deserved rest. Lately, it was not uncommon for fatigue to drain him of any capacity to remain awake, let alone continue with his therapy program.

But we had been briefed that an exciting event was imminent. Please don't fall asleep; not now, not today!

His face lit up with sheer delight and happiness when we delivered the news that two (as yet unknown) Brisbane Broncos NRL players were on their way to visit him. If only we could have bottled his joy.

It remains a priceless memory. Players Andrew McCullough and Greg Eden spent around half an hour with Samuel, their genuine enthusiasm and interest erasing any thoughts that their visit might be a sanitised PR exercise. They autographed the merchandise that they had brought with them, along with Samuel's own club gear, and were graciously good-natured when Samuel answered 'Sam Thaiday' in response to being quizzed about his favourite player. (We continued to hope for a visit from the great Bronco, Sam!)

It was a fantastic way to finish the day, and for a few hours at least, it distracted Samuel from his worries about a trache change planned for the next day. Tomorrow would be a challenging day, and it was with mixed emotions that we left our beautiful son that night.

Thanks to our Day 68 conversation about neurological pathways, Samuel already knew that while some aspects of his condition might improve or continue improving, there would be some lifelong loss of capacity—and that this loss could possibly be significant. While we still didn't know exactly what all of the underlying deficits would be, we wondered if Samuel may have known anyway.

Saying goodnight, we encouraged him to remember the great time he'd had with the Broncos—tomorrow would come soon enough.

But as we left the room, we were aware of the elephant still sitting in the corner, scrutinising us and no doubt wondering when we were going to have our next difficult conversation with Samuel—the one about life expectancy.

## Rehab Status Update

The rehab team seemed to know there was a void that needed filling. While we were coming to terms with the likely extent of Samuel's physical losses—mobility, speech and breathing—they stepped forward with the down-to-earth, practical information we needed to begin imagining a more positive future: information around spinal support and scoliosis, bladder and bowels, diet, reproductive capacity, mental health and social functioning. Far from being overwhelming, it liberated us to focus more on the future and not wallow in the distressing state of Samuel's condition. With their help we transitioned from a state of reluctant acceptance, heavily punctuated with anger, grief and exhaustion, to a phase of accelerated proactivity—and a growing sense that it was possible to get back in the driver's seat, to have some control of our lives.

Three months in PICU had given us a good understanding of how different departments in the hospital work together—or not. To be fair, while they do mostly work well together, each has its own focus.

The respiratory team supports breathing issues, often chronic, which requires them to take a long-term view of support.

PICU staff, on the other hand, are driven to save lives through an intensive, focussed approach. Their patients are frequently unable to speak, either because they are heavily sedated or because they are infants. Once their patients are stable, the aim is usually to discharge them to other wards for ongoing treatment and rehabilitation. However, as PICU is the only ward in the hospital that can support ventilator-dependent patients, children like Samuel will remain in the unit until they are ready to be discharged directly home.

The difference in these approaches led to several distressing occasions where the nightshift PICU physicians would adjust Samuel's ventilator settings, guided by their intensivist approach to medicine—but contrary to the advice of our respiratory consultant. On numerous occasions we were called back to the hospital in the middle of the night because Samuel was experiencing breathlessness and/or headaches caused by adjustments to his $CO_2$ levels—once on two consecutive nights. While at least one of us would always make the long drive back to the hospital, the drain on us was enormous.

Our consultant was working on a plan to slowly reduce Samuel's ventilator pressures to safer levels over time. While these pressure levels needed to be gradually reduced, breathing rates were a main consideration in adjusting $CO_2$ levels. We came to believe that some of the PICU doctors, while trying to make Samuel comfortable at night by adjusting his settings, were considering the complex respiratory formulas needed to keep a sedated person on ventilation alive. And it had become clear to us that Samuel did not fit this formula.

By this stage of his PICU stay, Samuel was neither sedated nor needing his life 'saved', and he could feel every breath and the slow build-up of $CO_2$. While too much $CO_2$ in the body is dangerous, it is the build-up of this gas which ultimately triggers our diaphragm to contract to take a breath. While Samuel's brain was getting the message from his $CO_2$ levels that it needed to trigger natural breaths—some deep, big breaths—his ventilator was not delivering this. If you ever played a game of 'pile on' as a child where everyone throws themselves on top of someone else, you will probably remember being the kid right on the bottom who starts wheezing to everyone to get off because 'I... can't... breathe! Get... off... me... Plea...'

Is it any wonder Samuel was so distressed?

In the end, we resorted to sticky-taping a sign to the ventilator with the word 'STOP' in large letters and pointed instructions to leave it alone—or risk a tongue-lashing from our respiratory consultant.

It was a distressing time. While certainly the different teams looking after Samuel had his best interests at heart, their different approaches needed to be taken into consideration and coordinated.

## In Sight of the Hospital

The children's 'pile on' game was the sort of easy imagery I could use when trying to explain Samuel's progress when talking to my mum. In January, Amelia and I had driven up to Mum's home in Hervey Bay to celebrate her 80th birthday. She was thrilled to have all four of her sons in one place (a rare occasion) and overjoyed that Amelia and I had made the trip—knowing what a wrench it was for us to leave Samuel.

Now, in March, she was keen to make the trip to visit Samuel in Brisbane.

Still very independent despite a number of health issues in recent years, she had saved enough to catch the train to Brisbane and booked a hotel close to the hospital. The plan was that she would call when she arrived at South Bank station, a few hundred metres from the hospital.

Jane and I were in the middle of one of our Thursday 'family meetings'— it was just a few days on from the revelations of Day 99, and there was a lot to discuss. When my phone rang and I recognised Mum's number, I quietly excused myself and left the room.

'Is that Craig?' asked a voice that was clearly not my mother's.

It turned out to be the voice of an off-duty nurse who, along with several of her friends, was comforting Mum as she sat on the footpath, propped up against a construction site fence about fifty metres from the railway station. By the time I arrived, the ambulance had already been called. Mum had stumbled and fallen in a pothole, partially filled with rainwater from the night before. There was a lot of blood in the water. A broken bone was clearly visible, protruding through the skin on Mum's ankle, which was being tenderly supported by the off-duty nurse.

Mum had made it within sight of the children's hospital. While we waited for the ambulance to arrive, I was at least able to point out the windows of PICU and exactly where Samuel's room was.

While the ambulance took Mum to the nearby Princess Alexandra (PA) Hospital, I went back to brief Jane before heading out to catch the bus that ran past both hospitals. By the time I got to her, Mum was in an ED treatment room, her leg in plaster, and had recovered enough to be telling anyone who would listen how proud she was of her young grandson who was in Lady Cilento Children's Hospital with a rare condition.

Mum had a bit of difficulty pronouncing transverse myelitis, but it was close enough for the young registrar who was treating her to know what she was talking about. Although she had not mentioned his name, the registrar had then remarked that she must be Samuel's Nanna. Mum was floored. Had news of Samuel spread like wildfire through the hospitals of Brisbane? It was nice for her to think so. The registrar walked in to check on Mum again, and said 'Hi, Craig. How is Samuel going?'

It turned out he had done a medical rotation at Lady Cilento Children's Hospital and had been one of Samuel's doctors early on. We didn't let this simple explanation burst our bubble that Samuel was now the most famous patient in the whole of Brisbane. In fact, another nurse who had treated Samuel at Lady Cilento also caught up with me in the PA while Mum was a patient there.

By the time Mum was settled in a room it was late and I had missed the last bus back to Lady Cilento by a matter of minutes. After briefly considering the extravagance of a taxi ride, I decided to walk to Park Road station to catch a train home. It felt good to walk, even if my route did take me along dimly lit back streets. On the platform, I struck up a conversation with another lost soul trying to make her way home from the University of Queensland. She was an overseas professor visiting Brisbane as part of a humanitarian research project. For too long, life had been going so fast I hadn't been able to stop and listen to anything else in the world, either good or bad. I was totally spent. On that dark, wet platform, late at night, I felt so far away from my family. And yet, for a few moments I experienced a surreal joy in being able to stop and listen to the story of another human soul whose world was so totally disconnected from mine.

In the days that followed, Mum had surgery to pin external rods to hold the bones in place and insert the drains that were necessary to remove fluid from the open wound. I managed to visit her every other day and we began discussing possible ways for her to visit Samuel in PICU. But a few days later, a social worker called to tell me that Mum had fallen on the way to the bathroom after suffering a stroke. For her ankle surgery, she had been taken off her blood-thinning medication and a blood clot had moved to her brain.

She would need weeks and weeks of rehabilitation and her health team deemed that this was best undertaken at a hospital closer to her home in Hervey Bay. Planning began for a transfer to Maryborough Hospital. In spite of everything that had happened to her, Mum was still disappointed not to have seen Samuel. And while she didn't want to be a nuisance to anyone, she also didn't get the sort of proactive support from the relevant staff at the PA hospital that might have made her wish possible. Our social workers did what they could to encourage the PA to plan Mum's move to include a detour to visit Samuel, but the best they counter-offered was for Samuel to visit the PA. This was still impossible.

So, there it was. Mum's independence was gone. The long-term effects of the stroke would remain unclear until her rehabilitation treatment was underway at Maryborough Hospital, an hour from her home. And there was no likelihood of Samuel making a trip to Hervey Bay anytime soon.

Mum never made it to PICU, and in due course she was transferred to Maryborough. She was sad not to have seen her grandson and disappointed not to be able to visit him to see for herself his temporary living quarters. I had tried to describe PICU to her once, but it was difficult. Her own experiences of hospitals were a world away from those of a modern-day paediatric intensive care unit, with all that it offers its young patients. While it is definitely not somewhere any of its guests would choose to be, the atmosphere in PICU is one of sacrosanctity, a sort of sombre respectfulness and even awe, born out of the lifesaving work carried out within its walls. And the professionals we encountered there were always committed to achieving the best outcomes for their young patients.

## PICU Unspoken

While I wouldn't recommend anyone eat a meal off the floor of a PICU room, I am certain you could do so without any qualms about safety—such is the standard of cleanliness. After a bed is vacated and before a new patient arrives, not a single surface escapes the attention of either the AINs (Assistants in Nursing) or the cleaners. Ceiling, walls, floor, ledges, benches, trolley, kidney trays, pens, stethoscopes, tubing, power cords, ventilators—each room is scrupulously detailed and prepared for the next occupant.

For most children, a stay in PICU is brief. Then there are the 'long-termers' like us or the 'regulars'—former inpatients with ongoing needs who may be periodically re-admitted for a quick check-up or procedure and then sent home. And there are those who are moved to another ward within the hospital to continue their recovery—like the young bone-marrow transplant recipients who move on to the oncology unit. For every patient, there are also usually several unofficial residents—the parents and family members.

PICU has several communal areas. There is a large open-air balcony with a scattering of day chairs that are often pushed together as makeshift beds. And there is a family room/kitchenette where cups of coffee can be drunk, tears can be quietly shed, and phone calls made to anxious relatives in the outside world. When using these spaces, discretion is the order of the day. Most parents don't want to engage much with others—certainly not straight away. To presume another parent may be interested in my sadness and misery (or even my hope and optimism) when they are nursing theirs, is really a top-shelf faux pas.

One mum, bemoaning ('OMG') her eight-day stay, asked, as you might ask a fellow inmate, how long we'd been in for. Our reply—48 days—left her stranded. If we had wanted to make the situation more awkward, we could have followed up with the news that we were likely to be there for up to a year, but it seemed unnecessarily cruel.

Even then, we had learnt not to use the length-of-stay question as an opportunity to compare how much worse off we were to other 'inmates'—

a strange form of misery one-upmanship. For some parents, though, we could see it was a sort of therapeutic outlet. After we had explained to one poor mother how long we had been there (about 58 days at the time), she proceeded to elaborate that her child's 'three days in PICU' had been preceded by a 159-day stay in a Gold Coast hospital. Like us, she was there for the long haul.

As long-termers we understood we had a responsibility to uphold the unspoken PICU code of privacy. Over time, even though we became acquainted with a number of other long-term families, we tried to balance courtesy and concern with a respectful, healthy distance. It was partly an act of self-preservation—we had enough drains on our emotional resources without becoming too attached to other families too early on in our stay.

There were times, though, when our defences dropped. Our hearts sank one weekend when we noticed that the young patient in Bed 17 was no longer there. Thinking back, we recalled that the day before we had seen a 'nurse needs assistance' alarm for that room—just one level below the red emergency alarm. We also realised we hadn't seen the parents for a couple of days. So, we were genuinely relieved to bump into the patient's father. He explained that they'd simply been relocated to a better room—one with windows.

Hospital staff are impeccably discreet. But in PICU, grief and tragedy are ever present, and occasionally it was impossible to be unaware that for some families their worst fears had been realised.

Once, late at night, we saw the tailored suits of the undertakers steering a bed draped with a red sheet. On another occasion, we glimpsed through the curtains of Samuel's room, family members being ushered by a hospital social worker into another room, two-by-two, arm-in-arm, to spend their final moments with a young child who had seen too few days. Though no one in the hospital had told us the details, we had heard on the news about a toddler and a terrible accident at a rural property.

Snatches of conversations overheard in the family room hinted at the other private tragedies unfolding around us. The close relative of a teenage boy on a ventilator in Bed 5 made a series of emotional phone calls, telling of 'meetings with doctors', 'they won't let me in', and 'doctors... turning machines off'. We had already noted increased security arrangements for the unit, with extra safety protocols for staff entering and leaving PICU, as well as a visible police presence around Bed 5. Perhaps recent arrivals to the unit may have thought the activity was fairly normal but by then, we knew differently.

One afternoon about a week after the young lad had arrived, the nursing shift coordinator, a senior nurse with a ward leadership role, breezed past our room, announcing, 'I'm just closing your curtain...' even as he pulled it across the doorway. 'Why? Because I can,' came the offhanded reply. His quick flourish had blocked our view of the corridor to protect the family's privacy and dignity as their boy's sheet-draped body was wheeled out on a gurney. We later reflected on comments by another of Samuel's nurses that not all days in PICU are nice. When we asked another nurse how she dealt with patient deaths, she told us, if a patient she had tended yesterday was not in their room for the next shift, she had learnt not to ask where they had gone. I guess we all have our coping mechanisms.

Meanwhile, the AINs got on with the job of preparing Bed 5, ready for the next arrival.

# More Bad News
# and Birthdays

## Still More Elephants

Samuel had done a brilliant job of accepting the possibility of ventilator dependency and issues around lung health, but I think he knew there was still an elephant in the room to do with his movement.

He would sense its shadowy presence late at night when Jane or I would be called back to hospital because there was a problem and he needed more support. Or when we would be insistent with doctors, trying to make them see that Samuel's anxiety wasn't causing his breathing issues, but rather it was the other way around. Or when we would reaffirm our love and enduring commitment to him each night. It wasn't something he could easily articulate, but his attempts to express his concerns and uncertainties revealed something of the very loving and considerate essence of Samuel himself. Spontaneous expressions like, 'I've been meaning to tell you, thank you for loving and supporting me always at hospital,' placed him in familiar, comfortable territory. Like any nine-year-old boy, he could be cheeky and even over-confident when life was going well, but when things were difficult and he needed reassurance, his loving, thoughtful side reasserted itself. Far easier to express his love for us than to scratch at the issues that were playing on his mind; whether these were immediate concerns about an upcoming surgery or the next trache change, or worries about what life might look like further into his future.

Of all places, we were presented with a watershed moment during Samuel's first shower. He was in his shower chair, waiting. Jane was talking to the nurse who asked whether we had a hand-held shower at home: we didn't. Here was an opportunity to open up a conversation about what the future might look like. However, having any discussion about house modifications would be to acknowledge the subtext—that there would be ongoing disability. What to do? Samuel had been looking forward to a shower for many weeks. And neither Jane nor I wanted to say the wrong thing. But as we watched our water-loving son revel under the cascading droplets, we exchanged knowing looks. We made an unspoken decision to let the moment pass, but we knew that by saying nothing, we had lost an opportunity to provide Samuel with another piece of the puzzle, to help him realise for himself what his possible destiny might look like.

While we didn't beat ourselves up over it, our conversation later was brief and to the point. We agreed that if another opportunity arose, we could run the discussion to its natural conclusion—whether or not we were both present. Each of us knew we had the unconditional support and love of the other to follow our instincts. While the outcome of any given conversation could never be predicted, we were united in our intent. I believe this was the make-or-break moment that would define the way we dealt with issues long into the future.

In the days ahead, it became necessary for the ENT team to correct the size of Samuel's tracheostomy—the surgical incision that had been made on Day 16 to allow the trache tube to go directly into the windpipe just below his Adam's apple. It was still a little too small to safely change his trache, especially in an emergency. The procedure required a general anaesthetic, and while Samuel was under, the respiratory team would take the opportunity to do a bronchoscopy to see what was going on in his upper airways. They hoped to find an explanation for the constant lung collapses, pneumonia and chest infections, and for why it was proving so hard to stabilise Samuel's condition. As a balcony party was planned to celebrate Samuel's tenth birthday in a week's time, the doctors agreed to delay the procedures so the celebrations would not be compromised by any surgical complications.

A planned fluoroscopy would still go ahead. This procedure was the final stage of the blue-dye tests carried out by the speech therapy team to determine the extent of Samuel's oral control and his ability to manage the complicated process of swallowing.

Radiology departments aren't designed to easily accommodate power wheelchairs. It took considerable planning to ensure Samuel could be seated side-on to the imaging equipment, which would track the pureed apple with its dash of radioactive barium on its journey into his digestive tract. The radiation risk meant that only a limited number of people were allowed in the room with Samuel, but from outside we could see on the monitors the blue glow of the barium in his mouth. As Samuel did his best to swallow the apple, we could see that the blue would go no further than somewhere at the base of his tongue. It would never reach his stomach. Jane and I exchanged glances that needed no words. It was as if the noises in the room had suddenly become muffled. Dazed and despondent, we waited as the procedure concluded and then made our way back to PICU.

Two wonderful speech therapists met us a couple of hours later on the balcony. Seated opposite us, they explained how they had spent considerable time reviewing the footage, analysing every muscle movement and contraction. As they started to articulate their conclusions, we motioned for them to stop. For a moment, we looked across at each other, four pairs of eyes glassy with tears, and I said, 'You don't need to tell us. We already know.'

This confirmation that Samuel was not functionally able to swallow would not be shared with him until after his birthday. One more elephant in the room. Things were bad already. Most days it felt like we were permanently bracing for bad news. But this blow was the one that nearly beat us.

## Happy Birthday

A child's tenth birthday should not go uncelebrated. The open PICU balcony was the obvious place for a party. It certainly served our needs. It was also where Samuel had been spending a great deal of time learning how to drive his power wheelchair, a model that allowed his seat to be tilted back and also to be raised so that he could be at eye level with the people around him. With the small amount of movement he had in his right foot, he could use a joystick and switches mounted on the footplates to manoeuvre the chair and use its raise-and-tilt functions.

His thoughtful guests brought gifts of cash. Samuel was happy to know his bank balance was going to increase substantially. Anything else would have been either labour intensive for Jane and me or an awkward reminder to Samuel of his physical limitations. There was a brief moment of alarm just before we got to the balcony when Samuel's ventilator tubing popped off his trache and went unnoticed by the health professional nearest to him. Jane and I both leapt to his support and the problem was quickly remedied, but it was a shock for Samuel—and a reminder to us that while he was surrounded by competent professionals, as his parents, we may well have been the only people who *always* had his best interests at heart.

As birthdays go, it was a success. His cake, decorated by Jane's Uncle Paul and Aunty Barb with a Superman decal, was cut (with some support) by Samuel holding the knife with his toes. The birthday boy enjoyed himself and showed the sort of cheeky spirit we knew and loved. At one point, when Amelia was giving him grief (as only a big sister could) about not being able to eat the corn chips on the low coffee table, he tilted his wheelchair forward so that the footplates slowly crushed any that remained in the packet. He still had some control and wasn't afraid to use it.

## Samuel's Courage

Samuel's birthday was safely navigated and the planned surgery was completed. The respiratory consultant completed a bronchoscopy, and Samuel's tracheostomy was widened by the ENT surgeon to allow for a larger trache tube. The first stage of creating the PEG (percutaneous endoscopic gastronomy) involved the gastroenterologist inserting a temporary tube connecting Samuel's stomach to the outside world. This would allow for feeding directly into his stomach and the removal of his naso-gastric feeding tube. In the days that followed, the surgical site on his abdomen became badly and painfully infected, requiring more intervention under general anaesthetic.

Later, the respiratory consultant briefed us on what the bronchoscopy revealed. Samuel's pharyngeal muscle simply wasn't opening. It was in constant spasm, effectively sealing his oesophagus tightly shut. This had allowed what could only be described as a cesspool of secretions to lap dangerously close to his paralysed, 'flapping-in-the-breeze' epiglottis, exposing an open airway.

These revelations, together with the swallow test results, meant we now had the 'full picture', and Samuel needed to be told. The next morning, we arranged for the respiratory consultant to meet our family of four to explain the final prognosis. Jane and Amelia drew close to Samuel, gently stroking his head and holding his arm. I held Samuel's right foot for comfort and support, feeling it flex and move beneath my hand in response to his emotions. And our consultant began. Calmly, methodically, each issue was raised and Samuel listened intently, eyes glistening:

- Swallow—ineffectual with pharyngeal muscle in constant spasm unable to relax.
- Trache—will stay with a size six as it appears to be the best size of tube and cuff.
- Vocal cords—are working nicely but their function will be negated by the need to inflate the trache cuff to protect the already compromised airways and lungs.
- Diaphragm—not working and mechanical ventilation will be required for the rest of Samuel's life.
- Arms and torso—not working. Legs—some very limited function. There may be some small improvements.

Although we had done our best to prepare ourselves for the moment, watching Samuel listen as the consultant laid it all out for him, tore us apart. Neither Jane nor I could find any words to say. In the end, it was Amelia who stepped up, asking Samuel if this was what he had thought, and gently reassuring him when he answered yes. He acknowledged that he had known for some time that he would never walk or breathe again, but that he had taken his cues from our conversations of hope—and, in hindsight, from our denials and unwillingness to accept the possibility that he might not 'get better'.

Relying on every ounce of sibling connection, Amelia acknowledged the situation as it stood, and then, with Samuel's permission, she read to him a list of his qualities. The night before, knowing what the day ahead held in store, she had made a list, putting into words the many wonderful things that Samuel was to her, to us and to the world—including the many talents and gifts that he still had and would take with him into the future. Among the many things she listed were his loving nature, good looks, and his ability to bring happiness to others. She spoke tenderly of his facial expressions, his ear wiggles, his intellect, wit and sense of humour. His intense focus on her clear, measured words reflected the true respect and love he has for her.

Our consultant gave Samuel an opportunity to ask any questions. Then she and the nurse gave us time as a family to grieve in peace. We hugged one another, gently stroked Samuel's forehead, squeezed his foot and laid his hands in ours.

Later, Jane and I accompanied our consultant, neuropsychologist, nurse navigator and social worker to debrief, leaving Amelia and Samuel to share some private sibling time. On our return, it was as if the atmosphere in the room had lightened—the last of our herd of elephants had departed and it was time for the day to go on. Jane needed to return some sample glasses frames to our health society after Samuel had tried them on, and a group of schoolmates was due to arrive for a visit organised by his school. While we waited for his friends to arrive, we watched TV and chatted with our wonderful 'Peasant' nurse—a favourite from Christmas and many other days—interrupted occasionally by other staff who wanted to praise Samuel for his strength and stoicism. Word had spread that the Thornes had endured yet another 'worst day of our lives', and that once again we had picked ourselves up and were moving forward, buoyed by Samuel's extraordinary courage.

## A Day to Take Stock

For me, Day 157 about a week later was a special day to take stock and reflect. The respiratory consultant told us about a new trache tube they had sourced that could potentially facilitate speech. Stomal review surgery was uneventful, save for Samuel's normal concerns about the general anaesthetic, which as usual, he discussed with the anaesthetist—he was becoming an articulate advocate for his own needs. A final round of IVIg had also been completed.

Samuel remained able to feel everything to do with his body, both inside and out—from the sensation of a full tummy, or irritating lung secretions, to an itch on his leg or an ache that signalled the need to adjust his body position slightly. He could feel sweat dripping down his neck as well as the pain of the medical procedures, injections, cannulas and catheters. He could feel all of this, but had no movement below C1 (the top vertebrae of the spinal column), with the exception of some muscles in his right foot and calf and a few in his left foot. He would never again be able to ripple and roll the muscles of his stomach as he had loved to do, or play the cello, or even scratch an itch. He would be in a wheelchair for the remainder of his life, however long that may be. His paralysed epiglottis meant he would always be susceptible to chest infections and pneumonia without the intervention of a cuffed trache tube, which cruelly prevented him using the vocal cords that had somehow escaped paralysis. Though we were crossing our fingers that the new trache would allow him some speech, he still wouldn't be able to sing out loud or whistle. His pharyngeal muscle spasm made swallowing impossible, ensuring an ongoing reliance on enteral (PEG) feeding.

And without a functioning diaphragm, he would be reliant on mechanical ventilation, knowing that while it sustains his life, it is also damaging his lungs ever so slightly with each breath it offers. A kind of 'qualified' life support for the rest of his life. All of this damage had occurred over just a couple of days—and 157 days on, there was next to no likelihood of further recovery. It was a few days after ANZAC Day, a date that has always been special for me, and I was still in a reflective state of mind. On the day, I'd recalled Samuel's commitment to attend the Springwood Service the year before, and how I'd been so proud to see him taking an interest in the day and its significance. A year later, with our lives unimaginably altered, the annual commemorations reaffirmed my belief that we live in the best country in the world. We have a constitution that supports its citizens, and our service personnel have defended the freedoms enshrined within it. Without it, we would not have one of the best health care systems in the world—and without that, Samuel would not be with us today.

Before we left that night, I said the words we said every night—that we would do whatever it took (or needed to be done) and that we would never give up. Later, I sipped a beer, hoping desperately that we could all be home together again soon. It was my 50th birthday.

# Homeward Bound

## Early Rehabilitation

Rehabilitation work began early in Samuel's hospital admission—and once begun, it was a reliable constant throughout his stay. Intensivists in PICU had stabilised Samuel and formulated a plan to arrest the nerve demyelination and to keep him alive. The following account describes the rehabilitation support that formed an integral part of Samuel's admission and treatment.

———

I don't recall that anyone from the rehab team saw Samuel in the first couple of days when he was in Bed 36. The focus at this critical stage was on saving his life, although I expect some form of referral had emanated from the treating neurology team to the rehab team.

Early visits from rehab after Samuel moved to Bed 26 focused on information-gathering and movement; testing and measuring the range of motion of his limbs to provide baseline data in case muscle contractures were to begin, as can happen with spinal cord injury. I remember being aghast that there was talk of getting him out of bed into a type of armchair—surely it was better to just let him get well (should only take another day or so) and then he'd be up and about by himself.

In those first days, moving Samuel was like transferring a marionette through a wire fence. It carried the risk of tangling the many tubes and wires connected to him and of getting them hooked on his arm splints and any number of other snares. The physiotherapists were hampered by Samuel's recurring bouts of pneumonia, necessitating medical interventions that would always trump their therapy work.

Clearly, work to get Samuel sitting in a chair would need to proceed in baby steps. Though I couldn't understand the rehab team's determination at the time, I eventually learned that getting Samuel upright and moving was central to his wellbeing. It would aid circulation and help to dislodge the mucus from his lungs. It also established a benchmark to aim for, to overcome being bedridden and focus on being out of bed—however that would look. It's hard to explain just how difficult a proposition this was.

Samuel was literally tied to his bed by multiple IV lines, urine catheter, cardio monitors, nasogastric feeding tube, and the vascular catheter (inserted in his right femoral artery for the plasmapheresis treatment). Adding to this, was the twin-tubed ventilator circuit tubing shackled to the enormous life-support machine suspended from the nurse's station. Transferring Samuel without pulling any of these out or causing discomfort was both tedious and draining, and it was daunting to realise that transfers would look like this long into the future. Samuel's discomfort and pain were palpable, which made pushing him to make these moves all the more difficult, no matter how necessary they were.

During the first days, when Samuel was in an induced coma, his endotracheal tube was replaced with a nasotracheal tube. The doctors explained that regaining consciousness with a breathing tube in his mouth would trigger the gag reflex. The swap happened on the fourth day. Progress it seemed.

As Samuel showed more signs of waking up—eyelids parting and mouth moving—it dawned on us that he would have no voice. The tube giving him lifesaving air, was passing through his larynx. We would need some new way to communicate—hence the tightly closed eyes for 'No' and rapid blinking for 'Yes'. It was an effective, if rudimentary, way of communicating, but for Samuel, it was also exhausting. We had so many questions to ask. So many things to say. We were wanting to answer so many of his questions, if only we knew what these were.

We used whiteboard markers on laminated sheets. Word charts and blink-blink-blink or squeezed-shut eyes to determine his needs. Holding the boards and charts in his view made our arms ache. It was hard for us to both look at the words and to follow his eye responses. It took a great deal of coordination not to be tripping over ourselves with the next question before we had an answer to the last—and that was with just our family.

My frustration got the better of me on more than one occasion when staff, needing to get their information or support therapies and medical interventions done, would ask questions at a pace where the inevitable avalanche resulted in confusion for everyone. Was he answering this question or the next? Advocating for a linear flow of conversation, while it was tediously slow, was the only way to minimise the frustrations of everyone involved. Even so, we tied ourselves in knots trying to formulate questions that would enable a binary response. And, if it was hard for us, how much more difficult was it for Samuel? I would challenge anyone to go a day when they could only ask yes/no questions or answer yes or no to any question and see how long they last before giving in to frustration.

We had no idea if we would ever hear Samuel's voice again, a voice which had not long before shown signs of being able to harmonise music in the same beautiful way as his sister's.

In an effort to improve communication, I even looked at the possibility of using Morse code. Thankfully, it was never needed, but I remain in awe of the man who created a communication system where the most frequently used letters were represented by the shortest combinations of dots and dashes. And his name was *Samuel* Morse.

Oh, for Samuel to have a voice again.

## Body & Mind

While it was all too easy to think about everything Samuel had lost, the rehab teams made a point of focussing on what he could do—working with what he had, in the hopes he'd get more. Although this approach potentially added to false hopes, we didn't care. We needed to be optimistic.

So just what could Samuel do?

Well, he could certainly blink.

He could also pull a bit of a face, and despite the paralysis that caused the bottom right corner of his lip to droop, he could make a clicking sound with his mouth. While the in-dwelling catheter meant we didn't yet know the extent of his bladder control, he had shown incredible bowel control, defying the potent chemicals of three suppositories administered within half a day, because nobody had told him the 'special pants' he wore would protect the bedsheets. And further down at his extremities, he could wiggle his right big toe—two inches of absolute incredible.

Each of the rehab disciplines has its unique slant, but to our eyes the different teams worked seamlessly together. Physio initially focussed on that big toe; on ways to strengthen it and extend the range of things Samuel could do with it. The occupational and speech therapists worked closely together on environmental access—how Samuel would connect with the world, and what devices he would need to do this. They also pursued the ultimately futile swallow tests. Early on, jaw realignment became an important focus because of some paralysis in that area.

Over time, the renal team determined that Samuel's bladder continence would free him from the catheter. He also moved to a 'bolus' feeding regime, where feed wasn't continuously pumped into his stomach, but set at intervals more closely aligned to regular meals. We became experts at discussing urine output in clinical detail and joked about using the Dulux paint colour chart to provide the day nurse with more apt descriptions. Instead of 'straw-coloured', it could be 'wheat' or 'pale daffodil'. We also became well-versed at using the special scanner that determined how much residual urine was left in his bladder after he'd emptied it.

There were more discussions about stool colour and consistency than I would ever have thought possible—but perhaps the less said on that topic, the better. Eventually, Samuel's body would settle into a fairly regular bowel routine—an important step in preparations for his discharge home.

The various rehab teams were doing an amazing job, but Samuel's state of mind was emerging as an equally important area of focus. After all, how long could a nearly-ten-year-old be expected to do all of the physical exercises, all of the speech therapies, all of the thinking, the wondering—the everything—before it became overwhelming?

There had been early support from a psychiatrist. At the time, we were still working on ways to allow Samuel to be understood and the psychiatrist seemed keener to speak with us than trying to engage directly with him using the rudimentary communication strategies we had in place. On subsequent visits, the matter of Samuel's anxiety was discussed, along with the possibility of using medication to remedy this. While we were not opposed to medications being prescribed for limited use at difficult times, the idea of an ongoing regime of anti-depressant or anti-anxiety drugs seemed unnecessary, and we were determined not to allow it. Essentially 'numbing' Samuel with more drugs might remove anxiety from the clinical equation, but we were concerned that it would potentially deprive staff of lucid patient feedback about the underlying issues that were causing the anxiety.

While the experts took quite some convincing, we could see that Samuel was not simply anxious. Yes, he exhibited signs of anxiety—including, a concerning red rash (an indication of autonomic dysreflexia) that could appear anywhere on his body—but this anxiety stemmed from a number of very real, basic physiological issues.

There was his anxiety about the need to empty his bowels and/or bladder. And then there was the very real distress he felt when his ventilation settings were inadequate. This could sometimes be because the settings were being tweaked; sometimes because there were lung collapses/blockages/infections; sometimes because of leaks around the tracheostomy tube; and sometimes it was a combination of these. But anxiety was not the cause of his breathing difficulties—quite the opposite. Given that he had no capacity to breathe on his own, it was obvious to us that *the mechanical breathing difficulties were causing the anxiety.* Funny that—can't imagine that any of us would feel anxious if we felt we couldn't get the breaths we needed!

Samuel didn't need drugs to treat his anxiety. He needed his complex combination of clinical issues to be managed.

We did, however, want to engage a psychologist to work with Samuel in a more holistic way—to help him harness his powers of thought and introspection. It was clear that the journey ahead would demand careful navigation of his thinking and emotions.

Plans were made for a psychologist to meet first with Jane and me, followed by a number of get-to-know-you sessions with Samuel. The two of us, along with the psychologist and our social worker, could then have a more formal, planned session to discuss Samuel's future with him. Jane and I considered whether it might be better for the psychologist and social worker to do this without us present, but quickly dismissed it as an option. How alone or abandoned would Samuel feel at what (we presumed) would be more devastating news if we weren't there? There are times, when as parents, we simply have to step up to the plate, no excuses, at whatever the cost to ourselves. We'd had a few of these times already, but we knew that these conversations would be a defining moment in our journey. We were bracing ourselves to tell Samuel that his future would entail long-term ventilation, as well as ongoing pharyngeal paralysis and quadriplegia. But we were struggling with how to do this in a supportive way.

Unfortunately, at this critical point the plan stalled: the part-time psychologist assigned to Samuel was regularly absent either because of illness or other commitments. While we made it clear we understood on a human level that such absences were unavoidable, as Samuel's advocates we needed action; a position we announced on multiple occasions including at family meetings.

A number of our support team members began lobbying the rehab/psych department, and in the end it was a senior physician who took on the role—a gentleman who also acted in a senior management position at the hospital. Having such an experienced neuropsychologist on Samuel's case was reassuring from a clinical perspective, although I was a little worried that his other roles within the hospital may detract from the continuity of Samuel's care. But after weighing up the pros and cons, and having met him, we realised that despite any obstacles, he was the right person for the task. He would be the 'First Mate' who could safely support Samuel with his thoughts and emotions on this unwanted and uncharted voyage.

So much had happened in the two months since Day 68 and our first emotion-laden discussion with Samuel about what his future might hold. Initially, I imagined that the neuropsychologist would want to work with Samuel and us, in collaboration with the social worker, to help clarify that future and work out the best way forward.

Instead, he sought our consent to encourage Samuel to work through answers to his own questions—batting them back to him with 'What do you think if X, Y or Z were the case?'-type responses, and empowering him more to take ownership of his situation, and his own emotions.

As parents, we desperately wanted to protect him from as much as we possibly could, including from negative emotions. But just as we needed the freedom to be able to plunge from one emotion to another, so too, Samuel needed scope to explore his darkest thoughts. Our job was to help him take small, successful steps to own the process; to let him work through pieces of the puzzle, without overwhelming him with the 'whole picture' at once. But we also needed to know how to provide him with the right number of puzzle pieces at the right time.

This remained a lingering challenge that weighed heavily on our already overloaded minds. Jane and I resolved again to support each other if and when any opportunities presented themselves for either of us to further the conversation with Samuel. We couldn't necessarily predict what his questions might be. But at least we had a process.

## Distractions and Learning

Even for those of us who were with him all the time, it was difficult
to comprehend the sheer amount of 'stuff' Samuel needed to deal with on
any given day: the stinging pain of the Clexane subcutaneous injections to
maintain his blood viscosity (thinness); the twice-daily chest physio; the
painful process of being transferred in and out of bed; the interventions to
hopefully arrest the TM (the plasmapheresis and IVIg); as well as the pain,
the waiting, and the boredom.

Distractions were a necessity, and they came in many forms. The
Periodic Table of Elements chart, sourced from Questacon in Canberra
and mounted on Samuel's wall, drew the attention of everyone who entered
his room, from the highest-level consultants to the wonderful Starlight
Captains who made regular visits to the ward.

These sharp-eyed, super-observant hospital heroes were on a mission
to dissolve the pain, the stress, the 'everything bad' associated with being a
child in hospital. When they turned up, they latched on to the smallest of
details and built on them to create what could sometimes be called joyful
pandemonium. Samuel's commitment to memorising the first 42 elements
of the periodic table provided the ongoing basis for challenges put to him
by Captain Genius and his colleagues. Regaling them with his marvellous
feats of memory took Samuel out of his room and the pain of his treatment.
It temporarily released him from reality.

The mix of mayhem and mirth provided by the resident clown
doctors brought another welcome note of positivity to the day—although
thankfully, they never did make good on Samuel's request that they source
the chemical rudiments needed to construct a small explosive device for
him, 'just for fun'.

Two other welcome visitors were Dexter, the beautiful West Highland
terrier therapy dog, and his owner, Tanya. Dexter seemed happy to ignore
whatever other activity was going on around Samuel, and his visits were
always calming and reassuring. Often, his time with Samuel would coincide

with a visit from a music therapist. Samuel would stroke Dexter's soft belly with his toes while the therapist gradually drew from him the smallest of decisions about a sound or a beat, or the name of some singer whose music Samuel enjoyed.

I must admit that when the music therapist initially arrived in the first week or so, I thought it would be a waste of time—after all, Samuel's broken body was hardly capable of tapping a rhythm, let alone dancing a jig. The therapist seemed like just another person in what was already a crowded room. Nonetheless, he persisted with his efforts, gently probing Samuel about his thoughts and feelings on the musical choices he was being offered. His successes, while seemingly small in scale, were like the slivers of sunshine breaking through the clouds after a storm. They helped us to see beyond Samuel's external physical reality, and little by little, see into his heart and mind.

And then there was school. As a teacher myself, I knew about the existence of hospital schools—years before, I had visited the classroom in the Mater Hospital, and one of Jane's aunts had taught at the school in the Royal Brisbane and Women's Hospital—but I knew little about the way they operated.

As it turned out, there was a school, and as soon as he was well enough, Samuel started having lessons from his bed. Working around his treatments and therapies was a challenge, but everyone involved in his case was adamant that education was a priority. The school principal introduced herself as Michelle (both students and staff were called by their first names) and she explained to us the foundational importance of education for children who are sick or regularly in hospital. While the medical staff do their best to make their young patients well again, if they miss out on too much of their education (and social connections) along the way, then they will be playing catch-up for a very long time.

After a long summer break where not much happens in hospital, Samuel's bedside teachers did their best to engage him—and they were persistent. They needed to be.

At first, Samuel was resistant to their efforts—at times he was virtually un-engageable. But both the teachers and Jane were insistent, and gradually it dawned on Samuel that they weren't going to give up; lessons would continue and bedbound or not, he would be getting back to school. Once he was medically stable enough and nursing staff were available, Samuel attended the school's senior campus up on level eight. There, his year five teachers found more ways to engage him and tap into his sharp young mind. It didn't take them long to genuinely appreciate his depth of knowledge and thinking. And with a lot of support, he was also able to work on his creative talents.

Wielding a paintbrush dextrously controlled by the toes on his right foot, he produced two frame-worthy artworks. Seeing one of the finished paintings for the first time, Amelia remarked, 'I could never do anything that good by hand.' Samuel quickly fired back: 'Neither could I.' That he could achieve something like this was another confidence builder on his road home—a home now adorned by a framed still-life bowl of fruit and a Sidney Nolan-style Ned Kelly on horseback.

## Chronic but Stable

As Samuel continued in the senior campus for the second half of the year, preparations were underway to allow him to return to his primary school. This involved extensive liaison work between his school and the hospital school, the teachers, guidance officers and principals.

In June 2016, he had managed to visit his school for a special assembly held in the middle of the day, but getting him there on time every morning was going to be a massive challenge.

The start of the new school year in 2017 meant Jane and I needed to be out of home by about 6:30am. Samuel's nurses aimed to have him dressed in uniform (or just about) before the staff changeover at 7:00am. During their 15-minute handover, Jane and I would continue with Samuel's morning routine—toilet, teeth, face, hair (particular attention required here!)—and then hoist him into his power wheelchair. The outings trolley, holding a back-up ventilator, emergency trache box, suction machine, resuscitation bag and much more, was packed and checked. As for other ventilator-dependent people, these things always need to be kept close by.

Once the nurse had the okay from the team leader, we would take the elevator to the underground carpark, load up the car and then I would say my goodbyes before heading back upstairs to catch a bus to Mt Gravatt for work. The temporary Education Department job I'd been assigned involved analysing data to better support schools when managing student exclusions. Having navigated the multiple loops and speed bumps to exit the hospital carpark, and Brisbane's morning traffic permitting, Jane, Samuel and his nurse would be pulling up in the school car park by 8:25am, just as the school day began. I would make the return bus journey to the hospital of an afternoon to help with Samuel's evening routine. Sometimes Jane and I would travel home together, but as we approached the time when we hoped Samuel would be discharged, Jane would often leave me to do the showering while she got on with sorting out the many details that needed to be arranged before we could take him home for good.

Samuel was now identified as 'chronic but stable', and the reality of discharge was looming. The hospital was ramping up recruitment and training of the team of support workers that we would need with us in the home. Soon we would be living in a hotel for about six weeks as final house modifications were carried out. The question now was what would be finished first? The staff training or the modification work?

Our own training had been completed many weeks before, allowing Jane or me to be the second of the two trained people who needed to accompany Samuel at all times. The two-person rule is partly the result of a complex legal mire between the hospital and families of patients under 18 years of age, but it is also practical: If Samuel needed a suction while in the car, who would be able to do it if Jane was driving? Having a back-up carer in case the first person suddenly becomes incapable of assisting is just common sense.

Here are a few of the things we needed to learn about to be able to have Samuel at home with us:

**Ventilator:** on/off, charging, changing batteries, changing settings for night-time, air filters, alarms and interventions, understanding basic settings—peak inspiratory pressures, peak end expiratory pressures and breath rates (these settings are pre-determined by respiratory consultants).

**Nebulisers**—provide humidification support in the dry circuit if required; connecting into the tubing requires quick changes to minimise loss of lung pressures.

**Humidifier**—connection to wet circuit with correct cables; spiking the bags that supply the water; positioning the height of the humidifier (related to the pressure settings on the ventilator).

**Tracheostomy tube (trache)**—how it works and knowing the different types of traches; inflating/deflating the cuff to correct pressure; preparing for routine trache change (every four weeks for Samuel); emergency trache change (for example, if the tube becomes blocked); using beaded chain or cloth tapes to secure in place.

**Cough assist**—controlled physiotherapy machine which provides breaths in a way that simulates coughing in order to aid expectoration of mucus/phlegm from the lungs.

**Resus bag**—to be used in emergency if the ventilator malfunctions or stops working. It attaches to the trache tube and the bag is squeezed by hand to provide manual breaths.

**Suctioning and suction units** –inserting the correctly sized suction catheter to the correct depth into Samuel's trache—irreversible lung damage can occur if done incorrectly; use, management and maintenance of the different suction units.

**Stomal care**—the permanent penetrating 'wounds' created for the trache tube and the PEG (feeding) tube require ongoing delicate care and management.

**PEG (Percutaneous Endoscopic Gastroscopy)**—deflating/inflating the water-filled balloon and changing the PEG (6 monthly).

**Day-to-day knowledge**—operation/charging/maintenance of power wheelchair; application of postural and therapeutic supports—leg splints, arm splints, wheelchair cushions and supports.

Without our knowledge of these things (and more), Samuel's discharge would not have been approved. Nor would it have been safe. Not so many years ago, a patient with Samuel's complex needs might have been like so many victims of the polio outbreaks in the 1950s, permanently confined to hospital and a life of social isolation. Thankfully, his support workers are trained in most of the skills and procedures needed to support him, as well as helping to maintain the safety and integrity of the equipment and supplies needed in his everyday life. Without them, we would have little time in the day for anything else beyond the immediate work of caring. Their efforts mean we have more time and energy left to devote to maximising Samuel's quality of life.

The road to home care had been paved for us by other pioneering patients with quadriplegia. Among them was Robin Cavendish, who became the first ventilator-dependent quadriplegic to be discharged from hospital in the United Kingdom, having contracted poliomyelitis in 1958. His wife's battle to get him out of hospital, recounted in the film *Breathe*, has all the high drama and tension of a kidnapping tale or prison breakout.

Preparations for home discharge these days are less dramatic, and more about painstaking attention to detail. Every moment of every day needs an emergency contingency plan sitting behind it. Sometimes things go wrong. The ventilator stops working, the trache tube might become blocked or a sudden episode of autonomic dysreflexia may occur. It is not okay to say these things can be successfully rectified 999 times out of 1,000. Put simply, if equipment and back-up plans don't *all* work *all* of the time, Samuel would die within minutes. Our lives were about to become a constant, ongoing risk assessment.

But everything was as ready as it could be, and it was time for the next phase of Samuel's life to begin. The most important home modifications were complete. We had a full roster of support workers to assist us, and all manner of medical and nutritional supplies were in place.

On the day of our departure, the hospital CEO invited any available staff and volunteers to form a guard of honour for Samuel as he left the building. Those who couldn't make it could follow along via social media posts generated by the hospital's public relations department. Samuel had broken whatever record there may have been for the longest single continuous admission of any patient in the history of the hospital. And so it was, to the sound of clapping and cheering well-wishers, that Samuel wheeled his way out of the Paediatric Intensive Care Unit and then out of the building to head home with his family—to *stay*. It was Day 480.

# Part 2—The Lessons

In this section, I have tried to draw together everything I have learned from our family's experiences that might be of some use to other families going through similar situations.

I've tried to separate these into three sections: **People**, **Planning** and **Practicalities**.

Some elements of our *planning* were very deliberate. Others were spontaneous, responsive—and sometimes we just got lucky. While it may appear that we had this blueprint from day one, we decidedly did not.

I recount our experiences of the *practicalities* of returning to *work*, Samuel's return to *school* and, momentously, his return *home*—how we did what we did.

This section, however, opens with an exploration of the human dimension of Samuel's story—of the many different *people* who were in some way connected to his journey. While it goes on to discuss our *family*, *others* generally and *medical/clinical* staff, I needed to begin with my own experiences.

# People

## What I learned about myself

Central to any relationship I have ever had, or will ever have, is me. That's not my ego talking, it's just logical that each of us is always the common factor in any relationships we have with other people. The way I approach others, the way I react to or respond to them, is all affected by the person I am. There comes a time in all our lives (or multiple times) when we need to stop and really consider who we are. The period of Samuel's illness and rehabilitation was one such time for me. Because, quite simply, if I hadn't stopped to reflect, and to try to understand, and adjust and learn, I would have imploded.

To be clear, there was no sudden epiphany on Day 256 where I suddenly understood all there was to know about me, how I interacted with others, or what positive personal attributes I could exploit or deficits that needed addressing. Nothing like it. It was bloody hard slog.

I have always been a problem-solver. Always looking to see how things can be improved, how they can be 'fixed'. Well, not 100 per cent of the time. Some years before I had found myself wallowing in despair as I navigated depression and my own midlife crisis. But as Samuel's treatment progressed, I drew energy from defaulting to my 'problem-solver' mode. I was the positive, glass-half-full kind of guy. Focussing on staying positive was one of the biggest single factors that kept us going. It would have been easy to give in to negative or even irrational thinking, but Jane and I did not have time for that. Nor did we have room in our lives for anyone who felt a need to share the despair they felt about our situation. Our emotional bank balance sailed constantly towards being in the red. We needed to concentrate on keeping it in the black, so that whatever small amount of positive 'interest' we earned could hopefully beget even more positive energy.

## Disempowerment

Early on in Samuel's admission, an overwhelming sense of disempowerment defined our days. So much was beyond our control or understanding.

Our first step to overcoming this feeling of helplessness was to harness our positive emotions—I liken this to 'accessing our emotional bank account'—and to direct that positivity at things that we *could do*. The main thing was simply to be there for Samuel. Beyond this, it meant doing little things, like fetching fresh linen and restocking the ice bucket for the cold compresses. Samuel needed these to alleviate the mixed-up sensory responses his body was experiencing, like the hot red blotchiness all over his body. We were also careful to ensure we didn't get in the nurse's way.

At home, late at night, doing the washing became a task approached with meticulous attention. Clothes, particularly Samuel's, would be folded ever so neatly. Pillowcases that we'd been given for Samuel, printed with galactic heroes, became cherished items and I would iron them with careful precision, with particular emphasis on perfect creases. These were small actions, quickly erased once the clothes or pillowcases were used, but they helped keep our battered sense of self-worth intact—and gave us a sense of control over at least some aspects of our lives.

The nursing staff were always understanding of our need to *do* things and for the most part we were immensely grateful for the tasks they let us take on, mostly relating to Samuel's routine personal care: washing hair, bed baths and teeth cleaning. But as time wore on, our needs changed—we needed respite.

For some carers, respite may come by having some significant chunk of time away from the situation. Respite for us would need to come in other ways.

There was not a single day of Samuel's 16-month admission where both Jane and I did not see him. Often, one or both of us would stay with him throughout the entire day. Occasionally, such as before and after my overnight trip to Hervey Bay for my Mum's 80th birthday, it meant a quick visit just to say hello. Making the effort and choice to see him every day was one way we could offset any feeling of abandonment he may have felt, and it was part of the 'whatever it takes' commitment we had made to him.

But as the discharge date approached, we were increasingly busy with everything that needed to be done before a patient with Samuel's complex needs can be safely sent home. We needed the nursing staff to pick up the caring duties that might normally be asked of a parent with a child in PICU for a short stay. While it was reasonable for staff to encourage parents to perform routine caring duties like teeth cleaning or face washing, the stress of always trying to be available to do these things added pressure to our already busy days. Knowing that staff were perfectly capable of carrying out these tasks allowed us to have a bit of a break. And after such a long time in hospital, it was empowering to be able to harness these respite opportunities—and to be in a position to choose to do so, after so many months of not having the luxury of 'choices'.

Though we might not have been able to articulate it at the time, in trying to empower ourselves, we were providing a model for Samuel. We wanted to show him how he could maximise (and insist upon) the support he would need to rely on in the years to come—and to help him feel comfortable to ask for (and if necessary, demand) what he needed, as he needed it. He has never wanted to be an imposition, so the idea of having people do his every bidding was foreign to him. It would take time for him to feel remotely comfortable with asking carers to do things, but regardless, it was important to continue demonstrating how he could empower himself and in a way which he knew he deserved.

I also believe there was power in acting with integrity.

If integrity is about choosing to do what you know to be right, even when no one is watching, then integrity can be the icing on the cake of empowerment. Choices can be big, life-changing decisions, but they can also be small, everyday actions. Sure, I could choose to just iron the front of Samuel's shirts and pants. After all, once he's seated in his power chair for the day, his clothes become creased almost immediately, and who's going to see the back of them? But I choose to iron the whole garment because I think it is the right thing to do. I have made a choice, and therein lies my source of empowerment.

## Spirituality

A generally helpful principle in modern society is that most people try to do what is deemed 'right' by the majority. As parents, we try our best to provide opportunities and experiences for our children that balance their safety and wellbeing against the value to be gained from that experience. Ideas of safety are relative, of course, so while some parents turn into 'helicopter parents', wrapping their children in cotton wool lest they be harmed, others are more relaxed in their assessment of risk. Inevitably, our offspring will get sick or injured at some point during their childhood years. If this illness or injury is the result of something we have done, supported, or omitted to do as a parent, then we suffer guilt. Perhaps it was our fault for encouraging them to sign up for the rugby league team or the motocross squad, or maybe there was the one occasion we didn't check that their seat belt was on. Perhaps they fell off the swing while we were distracted by our phone. When something bad happens, we question ourselves. We wrestle with the 'could've, would've, should've'. If you, or some other person, is directly or indirectly to blame for something bad that happens, then it is easier to assign 'fault'. And with fault, in time, there may come forgiveness. And acceptance. And peace.

But what if your child gets sick and it isn't because of anything you have or have not done? Then, who is at fault? Who is there to forgive? How do you become accepting?

I know some families are able to reconcile their child's illness with the will of some deity, but I really struggled with that idea. I found it easier to accept the situation if I saw it as simply 'the way of the universe'—and that, indeed, these things do just 'happen'.

I have had a strong faith for many years, largely free of doctrine and based on what I consider to be a personal relationship with Christ. But I am yet to reconcile the idea of 'God is Love' with what happened to my son. I remembered thinking, early on in our time in PICU, that if God did exist, how could He/She have let this happen to Samuel? What did Samuel do to deserve it? Were we being punished for our transgressions? Perhaps one day I will come to understand this better.

If there had actually been someone to blame, it might have been easier to find the strength in my heart to forgive them—to bring some closure. To find peace. But there was no one.

Throughout most of my life, my faith had added to my positive outlook and my resilience—for which I am grateful. I was happy to believe that there is some positive lifeforce, an energy, even some form of existence, which pervades everything, but I've never felt the need to explore further. I felt content to follow the doctrines of Christianity, because they are pretty good guiding principles for daily life. But now I found myself questioning my beliefs.

If I were to blame God for Samuel's situation—or indeed, seek to 'forgive God'—then that would require me to believe fully in the concept of His/Her existence. Besides, the notion of 'forgiving' God cut too deeply into my early Christian education and would have felt disrespectful to whatever the universal deity, entity, force or energy is. Any way you look at it, whatever that force is, it has to be pretty big and probably should be respected. I believe in trying to live my life ethically and with principles. I have tried to remain resilient and be more accepting of the situation.

And the situation was this: Samuel's illness followed the slightest of sniffles, picked up perhaps on that overnight school trip to Sea World. Should we not have let him go on the trip? It would have been ridiculous.

We were letting Samuel take part in life. No one could have foreseen, let alone prevented, the autoimmune reaction that would consume him so quickly.

## Grief

Denial, anger, bargaining, depression, and acceptance. I already knew about what psychologists call the five different stages of grief, so I was somewhat confused as to why I didn't seem to be moving through them. Or why, when I did make some small progress, I would slide backwards yet again. From a brush with depression during my midlife crisis, I had learnt that I had a tendency to cogitate too much over things—and to brood. I would play out possibilities and scenarios in my head, and this included imagining what life could end up being like for Samuel. More to the point, I dwelled on the things he could no longer do. While we always remained outwardly hopeful, dark thoughts about what was being lost swirled inside me. Acceptance seemed a long way off.

Then a social worker explained to me that what we were experiencing was *chronic* grief. I hadn't heard the term before, but it made sense. Previously, I had only really associated parental grief with the loss—the death—of a child. But I could see how this grief might differ from one where the loss is incomplete; from a situation where we were fortunate to still have our beloved child, but where his future was going to be so completely different to the one we'd imagined. And in our situation, there was no one to blame. Nobody 'stuffed up'. Closure for us hovers uncomfortably everywhere, without there being a clear mechanism for it to be grounded in finality or forgiveness.

The grief didn't really hit us until after the initial trauma and exhaustion had passed—only then were we able to begin processing all that had happened. But when it did arrive, it was often overwhelming. Most often, Jane and I cried in private, either together or by ourselves. At first, after a little grief session, I would try to snap myself out of it, to focus on the next task at hand; but as the extent of the losses became clearer, these little 'sessions' ran into each other. No sooner had I picked myself up after a bout of sobbing triggered by the sight of Samuel's cello in his room, than I would then think about another of his favourite activities; his tennis or his swimming. It was like I was carrying around a huge sack of boxes, each filled with something lost. Attached to each box was a range of emotions: grief, anger, frustration, confusion. When one of these boxes fell out of the sack, I'd be forced to deal with it. No matter how tightly I tried to tie up the sack, the boxes would still find a way out. No sooner had I tossed one box back into the sack and composed myself, then another two would fall out.

As the weeks went on, I became better at securing the sack. I even managed to stack all of the smaller boxes into one large one, which seemed like an achievement. I was pretty stoked to get all of my bereavement boxes packed so well—just like a furniture flatpack. It was heavy for sure, but all very neat and efficient as long as I didn't try to open it or attempt to make something with it. And temporarily, at least, it allowed me to get on with my problem solving and other duties.

When I explained my flatpack solution to a psychologist who offered counselling over the phone from Adelaide, her response was that I needed to 'honour my grief'.

What? I had only just managed to get control of my emotions, and now she wanted me to hold a special ceremony for them?

Reading this now, I am sure you are already a step ahead. The reality was, I couldn't continue to ignore my grief. It was raw, unprocessed and it needed attention. Only by doing that could I begin to make the load smaller. Looking back, I see this as the single-most useful piece of advice that enabled me to move forward, towards a functionally productive recovery. To take control of my emotions.

For me, honouring my grief, meant that periodically I would open the flatpack, take out one or two boxes, and have my little session with them. It may have involved any amount of screaming, sobbing, or swearing but hey, that was how I honoured it. I could then repack the boxes, always mindful that it was best to open the flatpack *before* it got so full it burst open of its own accord. The interval between needing to explore the flatpack has gradually increased. While some of the contents have been replaced by new issues, it remains important for me to continue to deliberately honour my grief.

## My Brain is Full

Never underestimate the physiological impact that a serious psychological trauma can have on you.

I've never counted all of the different alarm sounds we became familiar with during Samuel's stay in PICU, from the merciless, industrial whistle of the Hamilton portable ventilator as it started up, to the rapid, seemingly endless ding-ding-ding that followed the red emergency staff call button being pushed. Over time, we became experts at determining which of the various pings and alarms emanating from Samuel's equipment were routine noises—and which ones required urgent attention. Some of these noises followed us home.

In the weeks and months after Samuel's discharge, Jane began remarking that I wasn't listening to her. This is surely one of the most common complaints wives make about their husbands, so it is perhaps ironic that I didn't pay much attention at first. Only later did I wonder how many times she had needed to say it to me before I realised it was true. On reflection, I realised I wasn't ignoring Jane—more that I wasn't hearing the start of whatever she was saying to me.

I booked a hearing test and when I explained my symptoms, the audiologist remarked that no matter what the results revealed, for me, the outcome would be bad news: If my hearing was shot, I'd need a hearing aid and if it wasn't, then I'd have plenty of explaining to do with Jane.

Interestingly, none of my work colleagues had ever noticed this audiological anomaly. Just as interesting was the explanation from the audiologist: At home with Samuel, the part of my brain that processes sound and hearing (auditory processing) is filtering out all of the sound that initially comes my way. It is screening for any critical alarms or noises, as well listening out for Samuel's voice, the volume of which is limited because his paralysed chest muscles cannot forcefully expel air through his vocal cords.

My hearing was fine. Once the auditory processing part of my brain had determined the sounds were not critical, it could begin processing them as speech—and in particular, speech from my darling wife. But by then, I would have missed the first few words. It wasn't happening at work because my brain didn't need to focus on Samuel-related sounds because he wasn't there.

While Jane's scepticism has passed (and I'm sticking to this story anyway), I continue trying to refine my auditory filtering system so that only critical life-support alarms—the really important ones—are prioritised over other sounds.

## Problems in Perspective

We were learning to live with these alarms and what they meant, they were part of our new reality—both a constant reminder of the fragility of life, and signals for the many new routine problems that required our attention every day. At first, our new reality was all-consuming.

Outside the hospital, outside our home, it was difficult to come to terms with the way life *did* continue to unfold for other people, unaware of what we were going through. Deep-welled anger would often surface at these times. The injustice! I found it impossible to engage in casual conversation—the economy, climate change or refugees—I just couldn't care. I wanted to, but my focus was so different. And while people were enormously sympathetic about our situation, their understanding was largely hypothetical. Or that's what it felt like.

I like to think I have genuine commitment to issues of social justice. I am grateful to a former Head of Special Education Services who, about a decade ago, encouraged me to sharpen my focus in this area and develop genuinely inclusive practices at the school where I worked. Because of her influence, I was able to make sure a number of students with mobility issues had access to school camps and tours. This included, for the first time in the school's history, ensuring that three students, all reliant on power wheelchairs, could take part in the annual Canberra Tour with their classmates. This same drive and commitment—and the lessons I'd learned—made it possible for Samuel to go on his own Year 6 Canberra Tour just three months after his discharge.

While I am immensely proud of these achievements, reflecting on Samuel's tour made me realise that there were actually many other families living with problems and challenges not too dissimilar from ours—and that in many cases they had been dealing with those challenges since birth. My anger began to change to gratitude. Our family wasn't the only one with issues and we at least had enjoyed the time before Samuel's illness to experience the sorts of activities most families take for granted. I have many cherished memories from those years indelibly burned into my brain.

## My Special Place

When Samuel first came home, I found I was able to keep my emotional bank account in the black by carrying out the simple, routine tasks that kept me occupied and focussed on Samuel's needs. But I knew I wouldn't be meticulously ironing pillowcases forever. I needed something else, some other form of respite that would be long-lasting.

On top of this, I was still angry, floundering between the different coping strategies I'd been shown by psychologists. Often, when I caught myself having an angry thought, instead of managing that thought in the mindful way I'd been shown, I found myself ranting that, yes, I *was* angry and extremely pissed off. And frustrated. And tired.

And sad...

I had lost any sense of happiness and joy. And even when I managed to find some small moment of peace, it would not last for long before some other reality took over.

Drifting off to sleep one night, thinking about how bad things were, an image popped into my head of a place I'd visited somewhere in the bush. It might have been on the southern Darling Downs with outcrops of pink granite, or even on a cattle station in North Queensland. It was a calm day with thin wisps of smoke rising high into the air from a campfire and in my mind, I saw eucalypts on the gentle slopes. And just like that, I began picturing all the different and wonderful places I have visited and remembered fondly in my life. As my thoughts drifted in a semi-dreamlike state, I stopped thinking about what Samuel couldn't physically do now, and wondered instead: what if he could do whatever he wanted? In fact, what if I could do whatever I wanted in some magical place ungoverned by the rules of physics. I needed exactly a space like this, and so I created my own special place.

So many family memories are now interwoven with other real and imaginary events in this place in my mind, which I have created as my retreat. My special place is somewhere in the Australian landscape, with sounds and smells and visions that bring me peace. It is a place, free from the need or desire for technology, where the rules of physics are abandoned, particularly those that govern movement.

Early on, just knowing I had created this special mindscape and that it could not ever be taken from me was enough to bring tears to my eyes. In it, I have full and ultimate control of what happens.

And wonderful things happen there!

Samuel and I will float and soar above the trees, hovering and just enjoying each other's company. Below us, Jane and Amelia stroll along a rough bush track finding beautiful things to show us. A small fire heats a billycan, and the smell of eucalyptus fills the air. Sometimes, Samuel's power chair will be carrying him through the air until he gracefully leaves it behind...

You see, in my special place absolutely anything can happen because I allow it. I encourage it. I control it. I revel in the joy it brings. And I don't feel sad when I need to leave it to return to reality. I know I can return whenever I please, for as long as I need. Sometimes, it becomes a place where I can honour my grief, but above all, it liberates me and I will *never* let it go.

## In Summary–myself

- No matter how disempowered you perceive yourself to be, you will always have choices about something. Choices are often binary, and disempowerment lies not in making the *wrong* choice, but in not making any choice at all. Each choice made and each decision taken is a steppingstone towards re-empowerment.

- Even if there is someone or something to 'blame' for your plight, focus on having positive emotions. The decision to own your emotions is empowering and, after all, there's only so much available space in your emotional hard drive—don't fill it up with negativity.
- If spiritual belief works for you, let it do the heavy lifting. It has worked for me in the past.
- Honour your grief. It needs to be respected otherwise it will creep up and tap you on the shoulder when you least expect it. And when you probably don't want it.
- Understand just how full your brain is with 'stuff'—and the effect this may have on your capacity to process other things. If possible, try to make time for yourself to switch off from having to think, or make decisions. But when the 'stuff' does require your attention, deliberately plan any response.
- Recognise that while the nature of your daily problems has changed dramatically, for most of the rest of the world, life goes on as normal. Other people may try hard to empathise, but their understanding of your situation will remain largely hypothetical. Cherish everything.
- Practise some form of meditation or mindfulness. If it works for you to make something highly personal and individual, create a special, safe, loving and memorable place in your mind that you visit regularly. Keep it special and keep it safe.

## What I learned about family

While planning this book, I realised that it would never be complete if I didn't acknowledge those closest to me and the strength of our relationships. To do this, I needed to go deeper into my own story. And while I don't intend to turn this into an autobiography, I do accept that I am, at least in part, a product of my upbringing and circumstances. And more importantly, of how I *choose* to be as a person.

Samuel's illness has certainly forced me to grow, and it has been painfully confronting on many occasions to recognise and accept my flaws. I have never liked to let people down. I have always had high expectations of my own behaviour—mostly self-imposed ideals about doing my best at all times, coupled with a need to please others. This has changed.

As a child, my eagerness to please people was a sort of relationship glue, a means to bind myself to them more closely. In my adult life, at some point I came to understand that strong relationships can be about openly and honestly expressing your thoughts and feelings—allowing others to choose to *want* to be glued to you. But the idea of doing this scared me. What if, when I really said what I thought or felt, Jane rejected me? Self-doubt made me afraid that I would lose her, and without her I could not exist.

But increasingly, my need to please was being eclipsed by the anger and frustration that was bubbling up inside me. Already, the way I dealt with people outside our family had changed: I'd gone from being an affable people-pleaser to telling them my real thoughts, and to hell with the consequences. Largely, I just didn't care. I had other things to deal with. Then, even my behaviour towards Jane changed.

It is difficult to pinpoint all the things I wasn't coping with, especially after Samuel's discharge from hospital. What triggered me might vary from day to day, but certainly much of my anger and frustration centred on issues with support workers.

Having carers in our home around the clock was a huge adjustment. Jane had put in countless hours of work to make a guide for the steady stream of support workers who were now a big part of our lives, and I hated it when I felt her efforts were being disrespected or ignored. Unfortunately, the way I behaved in trying to 'protect' Jane was incredibly hurtful to her. I could be short-tempered, to the point of rudeness, when it seemed that support workers were failing to properly meet Samuel's needs, and my reactions were obvious and embarrassing to Jane.

Frequently, she would chastise me or tell me I needed to 'calm down'. If I'd had a better understanding of my emotions at that point, I may have been capable of modifying my behaviour. But no. As the weeks went on, I would shut down her attempts to talk about my behaviour with counterarguments about the manner in which *she* was calling *me* out. In hindsight, perhaps it might have helped if she could have asked me if I was okay, or if there was anything she could do for me, but frankly, why would she? I was being a complete prick—even though I convinced myself that my motivation was to support her.

From the start, Jane had always been focussed on how best to support the support workers in order to ensure that all of Samuel's needs were met. She was able to see that if a support worker didn't know something or forgot something, she needed to help them, because that, in turn, would be better for Samuel. I, on the other hand (and admittedly, it did depend on the particular support worker), would huff and puff when even small errors were made. I became visibly impatient at any hint of what I deemed incompetence or poor training, when in reality I was pushing my own unattainably high expectations—perhaps a hangover from my younger years—onto them. In short, I was thinking and acting more like 'Craig the child', when the situation required 'Craig the adult'.

I realise now that some of this behaviour stemmed from resentment. I resented that all of these people were in my home, but more than that, I resented that we *needed* them in the first place.

Of course, the reality was that we *did* need them—and we needed them to be good at their jobs. (In Part 3, I talk more about what I think makes a really good support worker—namely their ability to focus on listening out for Samuel when he needs something, consistent attention to detail, the ability to become 'invisible' to us as they go about their jobs, and of course, not falling asleep on the night shift.) But it is also true that my feelings about the competence (or otherwise) of various support workers were only the most obvious manifestation of a larger problem. Doubts about my self-worth as a person; my ongoing bereavement for the obsolete construct I held in my mind about the relationship I might have had with Samuel if our lives hadn't been thrown off course; and the overall injustice of the whole situation, all fuelled my anger and pain.

I am sorry that this is how I found out just how tough Jane is. I have always felt her love towards me, and I know my behaviour towards her was hurtful. But she was strong. At times when I was quick to challenge the status quo or assert my own thinking, I knew Jane would stop and reflect. I find it difficult to recall specific conversations but afterwards I always felt a sense of being heard, and listened to, and loved.

And our marriage has survived. In fact, I truly believe it has grown stronger. But my behaviours made for a dark episode in our life together, and not one I ever want to get close to again.

I have since asked Jane about what my change in behaviour looked like to her, how it made her feel and how she coped. While she has shared her thoughts with me, I fully respect her decision not to have her private feelings and reflections printed here.

Given my struggle with faith, it may seem hypocritical to quote scripture here, but a verse from our wedding service goes some way to explaining the grounding I needed to stay committed to Jane and our marriage. It comes from what is commonly known as 'The Love Chapter'—First Corinthians 13—and it finishes with: '...Faith, hope and love abide. But the greatest of these is love.'

## In Summary–family

- Return to the grassroots of how and why you connected with your partner. If there are problems, at the right time, respectfully lay on the table what's working and what's not—and then do your best to work through it.
- My personal growth has come from learning to trust that those closest to me love me unconditionally.
- Trust in the strength of your family and in each individual person's different strengths.
- Respect each family member's worth and resilience. Untested, you may never know what they are capable of. In a crisis, they can rise to a level you'd never have imagined possible.

- Cross each bridge together until you're strong enough to cross them by yourself—and then keep crossing them together because you *choose* to.
- Laugh together whenever you can—the memories, the moments— these times will be like gold. If one family member is struggling, find ways you can support them and help them feel okay. Ask them what they might need.

## What I learned about others

Because Samuel's illness was not the result of some traumatic incident or a motor vehicle accident, there was no media attention, no Facebook chatter, to alert other people to our situation. Although it didn't occur to us at the time, this privacy from scrutiny would later allow us to have more control of the media message when we were ready to reach out for help.

To begin with, family and friends only found out about Samuel because we told them.

My first call was to Dad, a quick conversation made in a small meeting room while Samuel was being intubated. It was nearly 7:30am and exhaustion and emotions made it hard to get my message across: This was an FYI call— we wanted him to sit tight until we knew more. We needed information and we needed sleep and in between getting these, we needed to update Amelia. In the waiting room, Jane and I discussed what other calls we needed to make: Jane's Mum, my Mum, Amelia and then a small number of close friends. Jane's Mum was also persuaded to stay put for the time being—Jane and I were of similar mind that while we would need our parents at some point, we weren't yet sure what support would be most useful, and whether it might be better to keep some offers of help in reserve, in case Samuel's hospital stay was more prolonged than we hoped.

Our 'first responders' were Dan and Madonna, two of our closest friends. Dan came first, straight from work that afternoon, and sat outside PICU and simply listened, asking the occasional heartfelt question but understanding that our answers were limited by what little information we had. His wife Madonna came on Day 2 along with their eldest daughter, Georgia, who is the same age as Amelia. They had questions too, but were more focussed on our wellbeing. They brought us three simple, poignant gifts: a glossy pebble etched with a crucifix; and two dark, flat smooth stones, each inscribed with a single word, 'Faith' and 'Hope'.

These three talismans became immensely important to us. On any evening, they were placed prominently in our home. In the morning, we would each select the one which resonated most closely for us and keep it with us for the day. Over time, it came to pass that we each consistently chose the same stones: Jane, the cross; Amelia, 'Faith', and for me, 'Hope'. At difficult moments, my hand would seek out the smooth pebble hidden in my pocket and draw strength from it. The power of having something tangible to hold on to at such moments should never be underestimated.

As the seriousness of Samuel's condition became clearer, a small army of supporters began to mobilise. A kitchen roster organised at Samuel's school saw regular meals deposited in the bar fridge at the back of our house—ready to heat and eat at the end of the long days. As weeks turned to months, there were school-organised hospital visits from classmates and an impressive array of fundraising activities. Others, looking for ways to help, made an effort to connect with the hospital staff through fun activities like a guess-the-number-of-buttons-in-a-jar competition, with a prize awarded to the staff member who made the closest guess. Perhaps they hoped that making a personal connection would encourage staff to take an interest in Samuel beyond the purely professional. Aside from providing entertainment for the staff, for us, such activities provided a welcome distraction from the often-gloomy news. Later, they helped to break up the mundane days and boredom that are part of a long hospital stay.

It also became evident that their activities filled a need for our supporters. While we felt helpless, our relatives and friends often felt even more so as they tried to process what was happening. Older relatives, in particular, seemed to view what was happening to Samuel as an incredible injustice. We recognised how hard it was for them feeling powerless to take away our pain, as any parent would for their child. Thankfully, it was never the case that the people around us became too emotional themselves to be of any help to us. They seemed to understand that we didn't have the emotional reserves left to support anyone else.

I learned that people might give in different ways at different times, and that this is okay. Being overloaded with practical offers of help on the first day would only have caused more stress for us. Likewise, offers of emotional support, however well-intentioned, are less necessary these days than they once were.

I believe there are two different components to support, and that these both exist on a sort of continuum:

- Emotional/practical support—ranging from purely emotional to purely practical and pragmatic.
- Timing—people are on a continuum themselves for *when* they are most comfortable to offer assistance. Not everyone should think they must respond straight away.

The sweet spot is when the timing of support offered matches the type of support needed at that time. I have dubbed this the Matrix of Support and I revisit the concept, along with my Continuum of Functional Capacity, in Part 3.

## In Summary–others

- Understand that supporters—family, friends and colleagues—will also be grieving and will be highly motivated to help. This helps to assuage their grief.
- It's helpful to have a way to update and inform large numbers of people—family and friends—to give them enough information to satisfy them, and to process and provide deliberate intervention if they believe they can contribute positively. Group texting worked well for us.

- Do your strengths lie in being a 'first responder' or a 'watch and wait' person, ready to step forward when needed? People can be either or both, so don't feel badly if you're not there on the first day. Your strengths will depend on where you are comfortable on the Matrix of Support.

- Supporters need to recognise their own strengths and capacity to help, knowing that families in the midst of a crisis may not know or be able to articulate what they need.

- If you're offering help, don't overload the family with too many options—they already have enough to process, so keep it simple. At the same time, open-ended offers—'What do you need?'—aren't always helpful. Try to come up with one or two simple options that can be considered easily. One of these options may be to give the family space and privacy, and to approach them again further down the line.

- While supporters need to acknowledge and express their own grief, they should hopefully understand it isn't really helpful to do this in the presence of the family. If they need support to process their own distress, that support is best found elsewhere.

## What I learned about medical/clinical professionals

Since my visit to the audiologist and her diagnosis about the root of my auditory processing difficulties, I've thought a lot about the alarms and sounds that were common in PICU—and about the stress they cause for the parents of young patients.

Some sounds obviously alert staff to an emergency, but others may simply indicate that a feed line is clamped or the temperature of the humidifier is too warm. As newly arrived parents, we couldn't tell the difference, at least not at first. Whatever the cause, the importance of silencing these alarms as soon as possible cannot be underestimated. In a perfect world, staff would be so attuned to their patient's needs that they would be able to pre-empt the alert and stop it happening. Perfect world! But at the very least, attending to them as soon as possible would certainly help.

Alarms, by design, are difficult to ignore: their pitch, cadence and rhythm can raise the heart rate and blood pressure of listeners, as well as triggering a surge of adrenaline. Hospital staff know which sounds are urgent, making them relaxed about attending to less urgent signals. But is it any wonder that parents can become distressed, sometimes to the point that security needs to be called? The stress can be unrelenting.

Today, at home, the stress of 'the sounds' continues, even if we are now 'experts' at identifying and processing the meaning of the various alarms that Samuel's equipment emits. Is it the oximeter signalling his oxygen saturations dropping below 92%? Or has the ventilator circuit been disconnected? Or is it just the feed pump beeping to signal that the bag of liquid feed is empty? In any case, we don't like any of them. But we know we must engage with each of them, even if potentially (as my audiologist pointed out), it is at the expense of personal connection with each other: 'Sorry, Jane, I missed what you just said then...'

And so, we have learned to live with the stress.

In PICU, we also had to develop strategies for coping with the constant procession of health staff going about their business. Some days it felt as if a directive must have come down from senior administration that all supporting health staff were to descend upon Samuel's room and his parents, all within the same half hour.

It was hard enough for us to stay abreast of any given update from the supporting teams, but when they arrived en masse, it quickly became impossible. A consultant with a busy schedule to keep would happily deliver a briefing to one parent, even if the other was already engaged in conversation with another practitioner. Our opinions and input were sought individually, even if the other parent was absent.

This wasn't a deliberate attempt to single out one parent—or to separate us—but it meant Jane and I needed to find even more time together to be able to share all the important details about what each of these teams was doing. And there was never enough time—the spare moments in our days were already pretty much zero. Initially, I think we accepted the situation as 'just the way things worked in PICU', but we quickly realised it was unsustainable.

Yes, the staff had their jobs to do, but the deluge was overwhelming, and we needed to manage it. Gently, but firmly, we started to push back—we became more confident about asking whichever team wanted our attention to wait, or even to come back later, so that both of us could hear what they wanted to tell us. Thankfully, most of the staff we dealt with regularly were willing to accommodate our need for some degree of control.

Sticking together helped, but we still needed time between meetings to talk over whatever new information we had been given—comparing notes to ensure we both shared the same understanding of what had been said.

And there was a lot of information.

There were frequent 'family meetings'—multi-disciplinary team affairs where members of all teams could check in and discuss the support and management plan for Samuel.

The format for these sessions changed as time went on. At first, they took place in a family meeting room, the same rooms where we'd received some of the earliest, most confronting news about Samuel's prognosis. Then, after a while, they were moved to the staff briefing room, a space used for regular ward round updates. And then, instead of us being present from the start of the meeting, Jane and I found we were being invited to join only *after* the health staff had convened. The first time this happened was unexpected and confronting. Nobody had let us know the format was about to change and it was unsettling. It felt like they must be having 'secret' conversations and so, of course, we wondered what they weren't telling us.

I also did not cope well when, in these meetings, we were frequently asked 'What's happening?' or 'What do you understand about what's happening?' Maybe, objectively, it was a useful way for staff to gauge our mood or to open up the discussion, but we soon became tired of it. We wanted *them* to tell *us* what was happening; what *they* knew. After all, were they not the experts? And, especially if they were having their 'pre-meetings', surely, they could update us, instead of it constantly feeling like we were updating them.

Eventually, these family meetings evolved to become informative, collaborative and proactive forums. The clinical team took on board our frustrations and fears about the change of format, and I think they came to realise that both Jane and I appreciated a structured meeting process, one that resulted in a productive use of time for everybody. As time went on, we also obviously had a better level of understanding about Samuel's treatment. As this knowledge increased, we were better able to process new information, and we naturally became more proactive in our role as Samuel's advocates and contributed to guiding the pace of the meetings.

Unfortunately, there was one painful element of these and other smaller meetings which persisted: over-repetition of the 'bad news'. I'm still not entirely sure why this happened. If at first we weren't overly pragmatic, over time we certainly became so—even in the face of frequent bad news. We listened, we tried to understand, and then we just got on with it. We had reached a point where we understood the situation and were able to begin processing the implications of any new piece of information immediately. We did not need the repeated reminders that Samuel's cuff needed to be inflated after we'd been told his epiglottis was paralysed; or that the plasmapheresis had not reversed the transverse myelitis; or that he might never breathe or walk again. We got it.

Perhaps there are some people who need to be repeatedly bludgeoned with blunt facts in order for them to accept reality, but this certainly wasn't us—we tried our best to deal with the situation as it was.

Which wasn't to say we didn't appreciate a bit of added context.

There were times, after a consultant or registrar had explained some procedure that needed to be carried out, where we sought a 'complementary' explanation, usually from the PICU nurse on duty at the time, to help us unpack exactly what that procedure might look like for Samuel. What it actually meant in terms of adjustments to his care, and what changes it would mean for what had become a fairly routine existence in PICU. We were able to grasp, medically speaking, any procedure about to happen, but it was comforting to have the real-life implications for Samuel's individual context unpacked. This allowed us to better process the complexities and adjust our ideas accordingly.

For parents of seriously ill children, PICU is a daunting place. Even cases far less complex than Samuel's can involve a bewildering number of different health professionals, all with different roles and specialties, and so it really helps if they can introduce themselves properly. This simple courtesy is of paramount importance to establishing effective relationships with the family, which will in turn help support the wellbeing of the child. Thankfully, in our experience, most staff made an effort to introduce themselves prior to their first interaction with Samuel or us. And helpfully, most also wore nametags, which made it easier for our overtaxed brains to place them on subsequent occasions. Over time, it proved invaluable to be able to figure out who was who, and where they fit into the system.

We were also grateful when staff were observant, picking up cues from Samuel and us in their efforts to lay the foundations for positive, productive conversations. I recall an occasion in late March 2016, when our lead PICU consultant remarked to a registrar, who was just starting a new rotation, that you could learn things about a patient by looking around their room. His eyes had just been caught by a poster of the periodic table that was hanging on Samuel's wall. A laminated copy of that poster—signed by Samuel using his foot—would later find its way into this consultant's home study, presented as a small token of our thanks.

## In Summary—medical/clinical professionals

- **Alarms**—Remember that families of patients have no way of knowing the difference between the alarms made by a feed pump or a ventilator. To them, all alarms *must* be important—or else why would a machine have them? Attending to them as soon as possible can help alleviate parental distress.

- **All at once**—If possible, minimise the number of people focussed on the child, or having conversations with the parents, at any given point in time. While it may be routine medical practice for you, parents need time to process *all* of the different information they are receiving from different teams.

- **Family meetings**—Determine the approach to be taken in family meetings. Sudden changes to routines can be unsettling for parents if not properly explained. Try to take your cues from the parents— there are times when enquiries about their emotional wellbeing may be welcome, but sometimes honest, factual updates are more valuable.

- **Know when to get on with it**—Don't bludgeon families with the same bad news time and time again. Even if they are struggling to process everything that has happened or that may happen, they don't need constant reminders of how bad things might be.

- **Practical implications**—Explanations by the experts will cover off adequately on the technical side of any procedure. Explanations in simple terms about what any given procedure might look like, sound like, or feel like, *and how it might be different from others that have preceded it*, is what parents need.

- **Maximising patient connection**—Educate long-stay families on the structure of the hospital, its different departments and staff hierarchies. And don't presume they know or will remember your name. Draw as much information as you can from the environment within the patient's room. It can be a window into their world.

# Planning

## Hope Remained

When we first made our nightly pledge to Samuel to do 'whatever it takes', we had no idea what fulfilling that pledge would mean, or what it would require us to do.

Once he was deemed 'chronic but stable', we needed to begin planning for his future in earnest.

I was torn. My heart was telling me I should just be with him, giving him the day-to-day support he needed, while my head was saying we needed to get organised for the future. Guilt would creep in any time I started to think about practical longer-term solutions to issues that confronted us today. It seemed an admission of defeat—an acknowledgement that Samuel's condition would not improve.

And that was hard. He couldn't stay this way for the rest of his life, could he? Surely not. I always held hope that Samuel's condition would improve, but in the meantime, plans to support him needed to be put in place.

Only in hindsight could I really call our activity, 'planning'. At the time, it felt more like throwing a bunch of ingredients—knowledge, emotion, hopes, opportunities and practicalities—into a huge melting pot to try to make sense of all of it and work out what needed to be done. If that is 'planning', then so be it.

I will also say, this was not us abandoning hope. However difficult it felt, it was a vitally important part of 'doing whatever it took'—fulfilling our pledge to Samuel.

Many of the solutions would be for as-yet-unknown needs. Our goals in the short-term were clear: getting back to school, work and getting home. I talk more about these in 'Practicalities', later in this section. Our medium- and long-term goals were less clear, but involved a lot of trying different 'doors'. The nature and extent of Samuel's disability meant many doors were sealed shut to us; we needed to figure out through which doors we could still pass. We also needed to know how we could do more than just salvage something positive from our family crisis in the long term.

If our goal was to maximise Samuel's opportunities into the future, then serious consideration needed to be given to what that involved—and how we were going to do it.

## Early Messaging

To begin with, Samuel's situation was private. If he'd been the victim of a horrible accident there would have been news stories and media interest. But as it was, there was no announcement to the world that his life had been upended so completely. Later, as word of the extent of his illness got out, his plight attracted an outpouring of sympathy and grief, as well as offers of help and donations of money. But for the moment, that anonymity shielded us. It gave us time to process the unfolding events and allowed us to focus on being exactly where we needed to be, in body, heart and mind.

It also allowed us to better control the release of information. More by good luck than good planning, the text messages we sent to immediate family and friends fuelled a manageable support response. While these early texts probably downplayed the gravity of the situation, keeping the information simple made it easier for our supporters to see what we needed at that moment—practical help with meals, car-parking expenses, routine domestic tasks and more. Frequently, this happened without us even asking, because mostly we couldn't.

As the days went by, more people reached out to us, most often by text message. They seemed to realise that texts were better because we could respond to them at our convenience. A phone call might come at an awkward moment and was liable to end abruptly if Samuel needed us, or a consultant wanted to speak with us.

While they waited and hoped, people looked for particular ways to help. We were limited in our capacity to give detailed responses to individual texts, but people seemed able to 'read between the lines' and come up with prompt, solutions-driven ideas for how they could help.

The community-minded assistance from Samuel's primary school, Springwood Road State School, was enormous, both in terms of personal support and fundraising efforts. Staff, parents and children joined forces to organise election-day barbecues (and invited TV journalists), cake stalls, raffles and more.

They set up a GoFundMe page, and for many months their food roster ensured we had a regular supply of hot meals to come home to at the end of the day. Our trusty old bar fridge was moved to the back of the house, and on a Friday evening, we would arrive home to discover it had been filled with something delicious. Every meal felt like an act of love and support. And as each day blurred into the next, these weekly deliveries also helped to mark the weeks. Along with other recurring events, like the Sunday visits in PICU with close friends, they helped us to know there was still a world out there, outside the hospital. By delivering food, they brought us emotional sustenance and a message to our hearts that said: 'We care!'

We knew that anyone close enough to know about our situation was close enough to trust, and we gave these people free rein to do what they could. We could never hope to coordinate their efforts; all we asked was that they kept us informed about what was going on, in case we were asked, and so we could make an appearance at fundraising events, if possible. We did try to acknowledge the efforts of all of these people on our first website and would again thank them (some of whom we never even met) for all that they did. It wasn't just the money. The love and the care they showed us with their fundraising efforts were huge payments into our emotional bank accounts.

Family, friends and sometimes complete strangers harnessed connections from their own networks to bring in money for Samuel through a multitude of events, ranging from the traditional (cake sales and coin tins in supermarkets) to the weird and wonderful (Zumba for Samuel and Shave the Teacher's Head).

Their biggest endeavour, planned with the thought that it might become an annual event, was the trivia and charity auction night. Through the Queensland Office of Fair Trading, a small band of supporters obtained an official permit to fundraise for a six-month period, giving them the official green light for many activities including the first trivia night. Not wanting to further complicate our lives, they waited until they had a near-complete business prospectus ready before bringing us their plans. Giving our blessing wasn't hard. We trusted them and there was nothing for us to do except turn up if we could. The first trivia night took place in October 2016, and the whole family managed to put in an appearance, including Samuel, who, because he was still an inpatient, came with a couple of nurses in tow. Around 400 people attended, and the night raised about $30,000. In short, it was spectacular and the biggest of all of the events this group organised. All told, more the $60,000 was raised by this wonderful band of people.

## The Cascade Plan

While the cash was coming in nicely, some people were keen to give specific, tangible gifts—items that would be needed for Samuel's discharge and (later on) to boost his quality of life. We understood why it was important for different people and groups to be able to do so, even if at first we didn't know how best to manage their offers.

Community groups needed to be able to show their members where their donations had gone, and to give them a sense of connection with the person their money was helping—with Samuel. Fortunately, the hospital's rehab team and accounts department were able to liaise with these organisations and individuals to facilitate specific transactions. But we also needed a way to acknowledge all of the donations publicly; we reasoned that if people couldn't see what they were contributing to, then they would naturally become reluctant to do so.

We considered using a thermometer graphic, of the sort often used in fundraising campaigns. Our overall goal was in excess of $300,000, and we worried that a single target of this magnitude—devoid of much detail—would appear too daunting and unachievable. Specific, reachable targets would be better. We needed a way of showing the public how their donations were going to be used. Our model needed to be flexible enough to allow donors and groups the satisfaction of claiming credit for the provision of specific items. And it also needed to break down the fundraising process into stages, with smaller achievable targets that made sure the 'must haves' were accounted for in a transparent and meaningful way.

The plan we came up with was closely aligned to our overall discharge planning strategy, and acknowledged the funding sources of different pieces of equipment. People could see at a glance what was needed and how cash was being directed, and a graphic on the website illustrated the logical progression of discrete fundraising targets.

We dubbed it the 'Cascade Plan', and this is a summary of the process we used to create it:

- We determined broad goals and prioritised them into a logical order that represented the different stages of fundraising, or levels. The final level was Quality of Life.
- Then we brainstormed every conceivable need (and want) and assigned these to the appropriate level. Most 'wants' fell into the Quality-of-Life level, which many people saw as just as important as the functionally necessary 'needs'.
- We costed all of the items. Different hospital teams were able to assist with this, and internet search engines helped, too. But sometimes we were forced to make our best collaborative 'guesstimate'.

- On the website, we made a bar-chart graphic that showed a series of beakers, each with a costed item tagged to it. As funds came in, the beaker filled up until it reached the amount of money needed to buy that item, and then as new money continued to come in, it 'cascaded' into the next beaker, and so on.
- Beaker items tagged for donation by specific people or groups were shown as already filled, denoting that the item was already guaranteed.

The graphic on Page 93 is a simplified version of the original. It models the five broad goals that we developed, prioritised based on our unfolding needs. These were:

- **Mobility**—Individual and family. Samuel needed a power wheelchair, and the family needed a vehicle modified to accommodate this. Having these things improved Samuel's independence and liberated the family giving us options and increased choice over what we were able to do together prior to being able to discharge.
- **Accessing home**—It was important for Samuel to be able to reconnect with his home after so many months when everything in his life revolved around hospital. Samuel was entitled to be included in the process of home modifications. This goal would allow for extended daytrips home, and it required home air conditioning (for safe temperature regulation), portable access ramps, portable hoists and shower chair to support any bathroom needs during these daytime visits.
- **School preparation**—Samuel was accessing the classrooms of the Queensland Children's Hospital School on level 8 but was also needing communication aids and access controls—mainly switches that would allow control inputs into different devices—in this environment and also in preparation for his return to primary school. Having these items of equipment would improve his access to the curriculum.

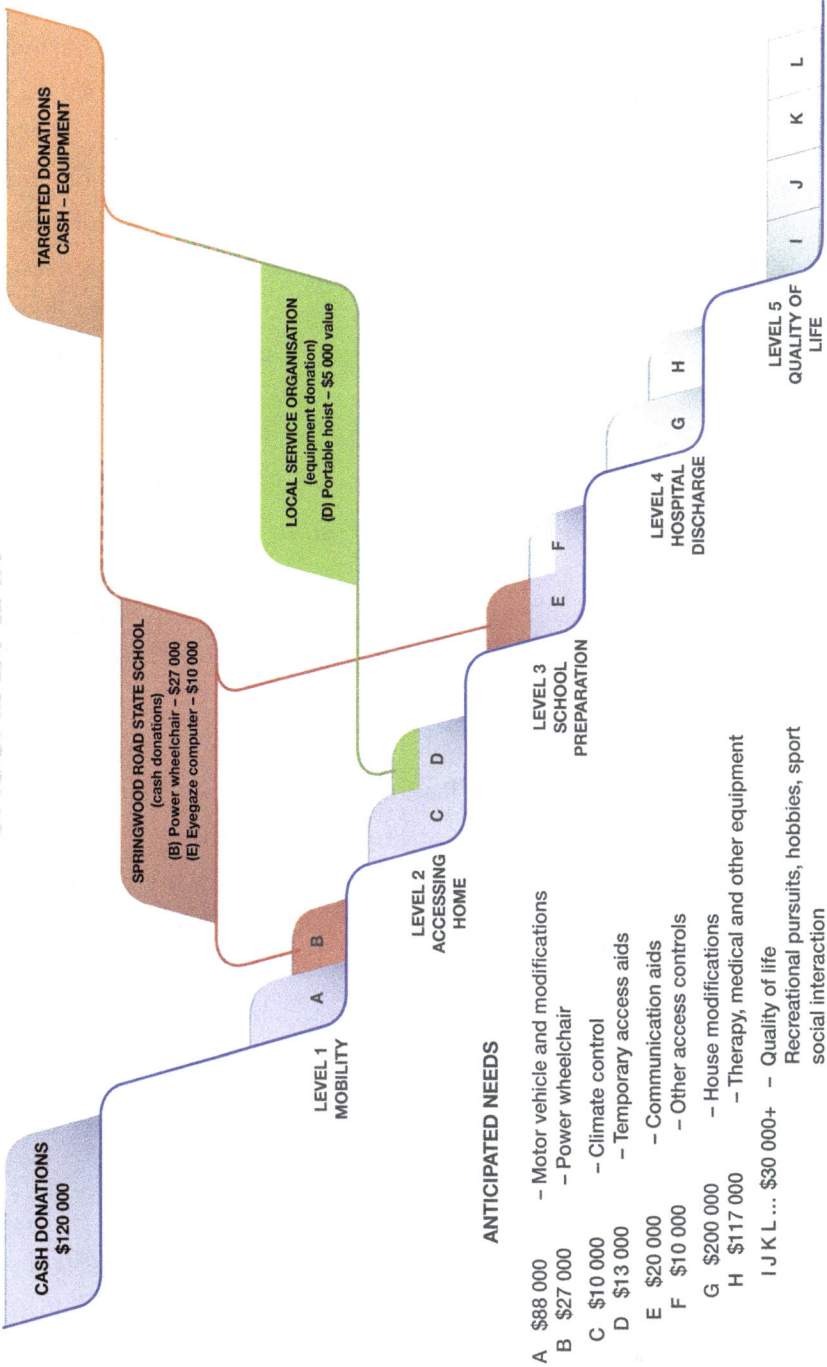

*Figure 1 This diagram illustrates the Cascade Plan at a point in time with an arbitrary income amount to illustrate how it worked.*

- **Hospital discharge**—This goal group was by far the largest. It included anything that was needed to discharge home, including completion of the basic house modifications, and vital medical and therapy equipment.
- **Quality of life**—Everything before this level involved functional 'must haves'. The goals in this final group were to be the icing on the cake—providing funds for adapted recreational pursuits or hobbies and continuing to improve Samuel's quality of life well into the future. They may have been 'wants' rather than 'needs', but they would also make the difference between merely surviving and thriving.

For illustrative purposes, the graphic consolidates the original multiple items listed in each group into just two. The two tagged donor groups are there to highlight how the plan operated—in reality there were many more. (Scan the code to access the original graphic for more details.)

*Cascade Plan– Original Website*

If we had been making the plan after the NDIS rollout, I expect we also would have included it as an organisation that was tagging specific funds or donations.

Though the cascade concept suggested a fairly linear process, at some points tracking donations became a little chaotic. If donations for specific items came in before they were needed, they still needed to be managed and logged. But that was okay. We were just grateful for the community's generosity. And the plan helped me to comprehend the enormity of what was needed and simplified these needs into manageable chunks. Because of this, it didn't feel as overwhelming.

## Advocacy—Government

In January 2016, serendipity called with an opportunity. Des Hardman, the radiographer who had carried out Samuel's MRI at Logan Hospital, was running as a candidate for the federal seat of Forde. He left a flier in our letterbox for a community forum at the local hotel that would focus on federal health issues and funding. It was set for a time when we might not normally have been home from the hospital, but on this day, we took an early mark—Samuel's circumstances that evening permitted this luxury—and I made a spur-of-the-moment decision to go along.

Des's guest speaker was the state health minister, the Hon. Cameron Dick. Before his speech, he mingled with guests and in due course approached myself and the two other locals I'd been chatting with. I waited as the minister spoke to one of my companions, trying to appear patient. But perhaps he noticed my focus on him, or that my eyes were starting to well up, because after a while, he extricated himself from the conversation and turned his attention to me. We introduced ourselves, and fighting back tears, I briefly explained our situation and then asked him: How is the government going to ensure that my son has all the support he needs to leave hospital and into the future?

Even before I had finished my question, he had gestured for his assistant to join us. We spoke for a while longer, the minister offering his genuine well wishes and vowing that the government would do something. His assistant took more details from me and promised that the minister would get back to me. And he did, personally. He telephoned me about a week or so after our meeting, just as I was driving into the carport one evening. We spoke at length. He sounded genuine and trustworthy, and our discussion gave me enormous hope.

From there, the mechanics of government took over. I emailed a written request to his office, and received the standard 'Thank you, we have received your email...' in response. And then we waited. And waited. And waited...

Fortunately, we heard via the hospital, that wheels were turning behind the scenes: The minister's office had requested briefs from the relevant hospital staff and these people were preparing their responses. I felt grateful and expressed this on occasions with the hospital staff. I knew they were under the pump to get these briefs done, and I know they knew it was for Samuel.

As it happened, approval was granted, prior to discharge, for the purchase of some of the equipment that would be required. It was a timely boost to the coffers, and meant we could direct money from some of the 'beakers' towards other needs. More importantly, approval was also granted to fund the support staff we would require to assist us 24/7 into the future. This was a huge step forward, not just because of the amount of funding, but because of the speed with which it had been approved. No one at the hospital had ever seen this 'Hospital in the Home' type of funding approved so quickly. They attributed it to the effectiveness of our advocacy efforts, something in which we were supported by the media.

## Harnessing the Media

By autumn 2016, momentum was building. We'd endured the most devastating news about Samuel's prognosis, and moved on. We had a clearer picture in our minds of what needed to be done for the longer term, and that meant it was time to share our story publicly.

Figuring we likely only had one main shot at this, we wanted as much to be set up in the background as possible: a website, an online fundraising platform, the Cascade Plan, and an established Facebook following were all important if we were to maximise the value of any media 'exposure'. Already, through our regular group text message updates, we had a means to share information with a wide circle of friends, relatives and supporters, and Jane was committed to maintaining this communication route.

These weekly missives were going out to well over a hundred people, who were passing on news to their own families—and from them, on into the wider community. It meant we could keep people in the loop without needing to be constantly telephoning, emailing and texting individuals. It took the pressure off us and meant we had at least some time at night to regroup.

We also took advantage of Samuel's move to Bed 3 on the 'Riverside' half of PICU, arranging a collection of handmade cards from Samuel's classmates on the three window panels facing towards South Bank Parklands so that

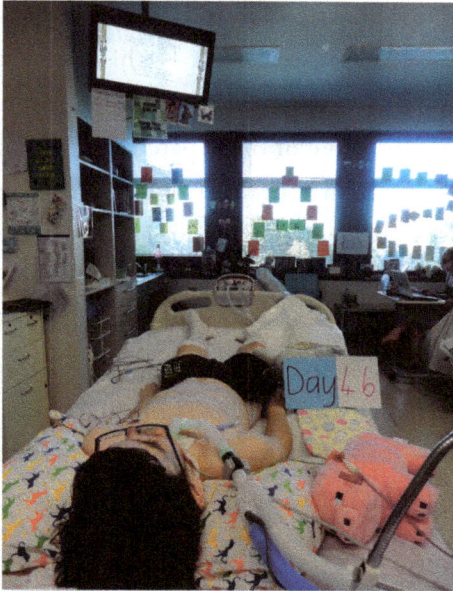

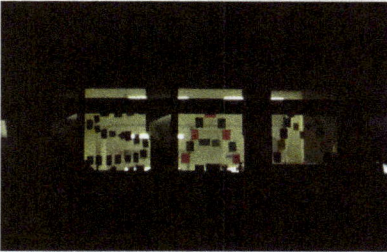

*S-A-M was spelled out in the window. Q-L-D for State of Origin and M-U-M for Mother's Day*

they spelt out 'S-A-M'. They were clearly visible to passers-by, especially at night when the lights from Bed 3 were on, and it was heart-warming to hear from people who'd seen them. For Mother's Day 2016, Samuel conspired with Amelia and me to rearrange the cards to make it the neatest 'M-U-M' you could see from South Bank—a simple moment of pleasure for Jane in what was a particularly difficult month.

All of this laid the groundwork for what came next.

Plans were in place to go public with our story, but one significant concern weighed on my mind. As fun as he is to be around, Samuel is actually quite shy. He shuns attention and is uncomfortable in the spotlight. Whether this shyness has been exacerbated by his circumstances, or whether it would have emerged as an inherent part of his personality as he grew, I've never been certain. It was one of those parenting moments when you just know your view of what is in your child's best interests may not be in sync with their own ideas on the matter, and that whatever choices you make could have consequences.

We convinced Samuel it needed to be done, but in the months and years since then, we have always sought to acknowledge any discomfort he expresses and to shield him from anything he really doesn't want to do. In late 2016, for example, he declined a request from the hospital PR department to take part in the fun final grab of a promotional video they were making. Being allowed to say 'no' was empowering—indeed, we all felt a little more empowered by his decision. There were no hard feelings: the PR team solved their problem, and the world went on.

The hospital's wonderful media team started to put out feelers to the national TV networks but initially came up cold. Our timing was unfortunate. Just when we were ready to step forward, one of the main networks was focussed on the story of a teenage rugby league player who had suffered a serious spinal cord injury, and his enormous funding and recovery needs. The story ran across two weeks, airing just prior to weekend football telecasts. The media team were a little surprised by the lack of interest in Samuel's story, but undaunted, they cast their net wider and came up trumps with Janelle Miles, a journalist writing on health topics for the Insight section of Brisbane's *Courier Mail*. On Saturday 29 May 2016, Samuel's story hit the press. Janelle's article, headlined Fight of His Life, was magnificent, hitting the hearts of readers young and old.

Later, Channel Nine ran a segment on Samuel in their nightly news. Channel Seven aired a story on my then 83-year-old father Eric, who was trekking the Camino Frances, from St Jean Pied du Port in France to Santiago de Compostela in Spain, to raise awareness and funds for his grandson's care. It would have been a feat in itself—especially given his age and the multiple health challenges he'd faced in the past decade or two—but this would be the third time in eight years that Samuel's Poppy had made the 769km journey. In Santiago, he planned to ensure Samuel's name was inscribed on the certificate of completion, along with his own.

The cameraman sent to film the segment was stunned to be told it was in aid of a boy who had contracted transverse myelitis. In a strange coincidence, he had survived his own brush with this disorder a decade earlier. Unlike Samuel, he had recovered with only the slightest residual nerve damage in one leg—one of the lucky 'one-third' of cases.

## Celebrities

Balancing Samuel's desire for privacy with the need to generate the public goodwill necessary to drive fundraising was frequently challenging. Sometimes, he was happy to take part in a media opportunity, but at other times he was reluctant and occasionally turned the attention down altogether.

The hospital was frequently visited by all manner of celebrities, and with a family's permission, footage or pictures of these visits could be released to the media—valuable publicity for both the hospital and its famous visitors. While he was thrilled to meet his favourite Brisbane Broncos players, Samuel proved harder to impress when Hollywood came knocking. On one occasion he declined a chance to meet Chris Hemsworth and Tom Hiddleston—he just didn't feel like it.

A few days previously, his mum and big sister had been thrilled to be in the room when Taylor Swift came calling, graciously posing for pictures and taking time for a one-on-one chat with Samuel. While Samuel did enjoy the visit, he also later observed that if any of these wealthy visitors could just donate a little of their money we would have had all we needed to get him home.

Chris Hemsworth did finally manage to meet Samuel when Juiced TV invited him onto the red carpet for the October 2017 premiere of *Thor: Ragnarök* at Robina on the Gold Coast.

Where possible, we fed the media machine newsworthy snippets like these while shielding Samuel from too much direct contact. Social media was useful here; posting pictures of celebrity encounters boosted the campaign's profile in a positive way. It helped to have a teenage daughter who was an expert in the workings of Facebook, Instagram and so on, as we were pretty inept, at least to start with. And Amelia has a wonderful way with words.

It was heartening to see our efforts start to pay off. Online search engines were beginning to return results with details about Samuel's journey—and even now, a quick Google search will bring up the pictures of Samuel and Taylor Swift that graced the front page of the *Gold Coast Bulletin*. Fortunately, we never needed to lobby the Health Department, but it was reassuring to think that media awareness of Samuel's story would have made it easier for us to rally public support if we'd needed to.

Visits from popstars and Hollywood actors were all well and good, but they paled in comparison to the moments of pure delight occasioned by encounters with Samuel's rugby league idols.

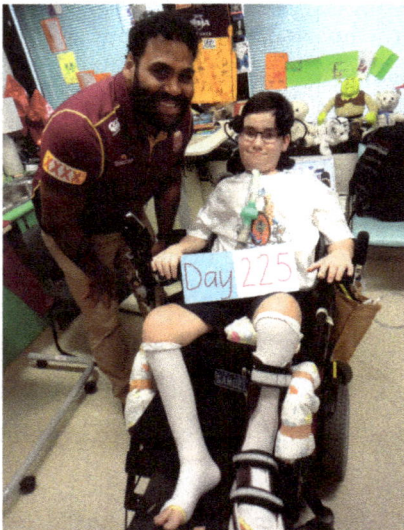

*Meeting rugby league hero, Sam Thaiday, for the first time.*

In July 2016, Queensland rugby stars Greg Inglis and Nate Myles dropped in for a visit on their way to the airport for the third State of Origin match against New South Wales in Melbourne. Samuel's delight at seeing them walk in was amazing enough, but when Sam Thaiday followed them into the room moments later, Samuel's face was a vision of joy. Tears welled in all of our eyes.

It was clear that Sam was able to look past the illnesses, the equipment and the disabilities and really see any children in a room. He spoke so calmly and naturally. He put Samuel and us at ease, latching on to our names like he'd known us forever and chatting happily until it was time to leave. If that had been the great player's only visit, our Samuel would have been quite content with the memory for a long time. Happily, though, it was the first of many meetings. Sam even asked to interview Samuel for a piece that aired during the 2016 Channel 9 Starlight Foundation Telethon. The pair has connected quite a few times since.

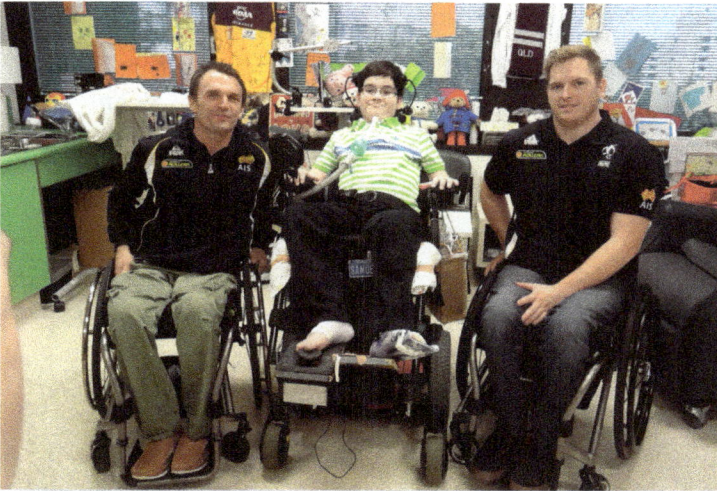

*Aussie Rollers Basketballers, Tige Simmons (L) and Matt McShane before the 2016 Rio Paralympics.*

Other special visitors were Tige Simmons and Matt McShane, both members of the Rollers—the Australian Paralympic basketball team. Matt connected in a special way with Samuel, having contracted transverse myelitis himself when he was nineteen. We like to think Samuel offered his own little bit of inspiration to the two Rollers in the lead up to the 2016 Paralympics.

## NDIS and Association

Cash steadily came in from the fundraising activities that friends, family and many people unknown to us arranged. We were grateful for all of the support and remain indebted to many people. But it was becoming clear we needed to consider how Samuel's needs would be funded, not just in the immediate future, but for the rest of his life. The newly launched National Disability Insurance Scheme (NDIS) had not yet been rolled out in our area and it wasn't clear what it would fund anyway. After talking it over with a few close relatives and friends who had some experience with incorporated associations, it was agreed that this should be done and the formal association, 'Campaign for Samuel', began.

Pivotal in achieving this were Jane's uncle, David Harwood, and my father, Eric. Harnessing their combined legal knowledge and experience, they drafted the operating rules, debating back and forth about the intricacies and implications of the many details that needed to be considered. After much consultation, the new unincorporated association eventually settled on the eleventh draft of its rules. There were 24 inaugural members—close relatives or family friends—with Samuel admitted as the first.

In early discussions, the members insisted that the rules provide an avenue of respite for Jane and me, as the parents who were faced with the burden of care. The cost of maximising Samuel's quality of life was going to be enormous, so primarily, the rules were about offsetting the 'necessitous circumstances'—a legal turn of phrase referring to the extra expense incurred as a direct result of Samuel's situation. The rules also enabled support to be extended to others who have suffered a spinal cord injury, especially where it has been caused by transverse myelitis.

Incorporation was the next step. The association was registered as a charity with the Australian Charities and Not-for-profits Commission (ACNC). It received approval from the Queensland Office of Fair Trading to fundraise for an indefinite period of time and a Deductible Gift Recipient (tax deductible) Fund: the Samuel Thorne Fund, was established. This may sound straightforward, but it was far from it and explaining the process fully could easily take a book in itself. That said, it was one of the best decisions we made, because it opened up opportunities.

The association would:

- Provide a focal point for family and friends, as well as other supporters.
- Qualify as a charity entitled to use the '.org.au' domain tag (as opposed to just '.org').
- Establish an account with an internet service provider using the '.org.au' suffix to host a better website than the free site we were using.
- Be able to access the GiveNow online fundraising platform. This crowdfunding platform is open only to charities with the '.org.au' domain tag, and takes a far smaller cut of donations than other similar platforms.
- Have free access to Microsoft's Office 365 suite because of our charitable status.
- Register with Connecting Up, a charity providing free or cheaper software and tech support to not-for-profit groups.
- Continue to operate well into the future, as long as audits, annual returns and other commitments set out in the rules were fulfilled.
- Continue as a support foundation for Samuel, even after Jane and I depart this world.
- Underwrite (if needed) larger purchases and fund supports that the NDIS won't.

This last point was the clincher. At the time, we could get no clarity about how Samuel's needs would be supported under the NDIS. Clearly, there was no dispute that Samuel had significant disabilities, but the state treasury funding for the CHQ at Home support workers was primarily aimed at managing his ventilation needs, which was technically a state Health Department matter. We didn't want to risk being caught up in any federal-versus-state argy-bargy over money. The Campaign's fundraising meant that if Samuel needed something, especially to support his quality of life, then money would be available from funds overseen by the executive committee.

It took just ten weeks to go from the first (unincorporated) association meeting to the fully operational Campaign for Samuel Incorporated, a process we were told could take many more weeks to complete. It was a huge win, both financially and emotionally—and we were buoyed by the strength of the support that was united behind our family, and of what could be achieved together. It was reassuring to know we were keeping Samuel's options open, both in terms of his future care needs and life opportunities.

www.campaignforsamuel.org.au

*Campaign for Samuel Incorporated - Website*

## Keeping (Cabin) Doors Open—Canberra

Samuel's physical limitations meant that many of life's doors had been abruptly slammed shut in his (and our) faces—much-loved activities like swimming club, basketball, rugby league and cello were lost to him forever. Other doors remained tantalisingly, ever-so-slightly ajar—the question was, could we open them or not?

One such door was the Year Six Canberra Tour, a rite of passage for children all over the country as they near the end of their time at primary school. We were determined to try to get him there.

As part of my job, I had been on many Canberra tours in the past, so I understood both their significance for students as well as the work that went into their planning.

I'd started thinking about how Samuel might be able to attend, even before it was raised as a topic of conversation. The practicalities demanded some over-the-horizon planning, and we felt strongly that if we were going to even attempt the mission, we needed to do our utmost to succeed. Not to do so, would make our pledge to 'do whatever it takes' ring hollow.

At this point it was early 2017. All being well, Samuel was due to be discharged in March—the Canberra trip was set for July. We thought we could pretty much do it, and, with all the other doors that seemed to have closed to him, we knew it would be a huge boost to his state of mind. And if we succeeded, a door would be wedged open—allowing the prospect of other travel in the future.

The only conceivable way to get Samuel to Canberra would be to fly—the usual route, an overnight coach trip via Sydney with his classmates, simply wasn't possible to plan in such a short timeframe. The initial feedback from the CHQ at Home service wasn't promising: we were told that a patient needed to be at least six months post-discharge before any venture away from home could be considered. And flying? Were we serious?

Absolutely. Now was the perfect time to demonstrate to Samuel that we were willing to move mountains to help him achieve his goals, and that this opportunity—air travel—was possible.

We knew it was a huge undertaking. Air travel for ventilator-dependent travellers is certainly possible, but never easy. Fortunately, we had someone we could turn to for advice.

We had met and been inspired by Perry Cross, founder of the Perry Cross Spinal Research Foundation. Injured on the rugby field in 1994, Perry became a ventilated quadriplegic at the age of 19. In 1996, he travelled to the USA where he met with Christopher Reeve. Famously, he convinced the former Superman that it was still possible for him to fly (at least commercially), and the actor later returned the visit to Perry in Australia.

So, Perry, what do we do? Among the advice he gave us was to pop out to Brisbane airport to meet the Qantas special handling team. Perhaps they were having a quiet day, or maybe it was lucky timing, but on the day we visited, the Qantas crew set aside what they were doing to give Samuel a practice ride in their sling and specially designed Eagle hoist there and then. Just knowing what to expect went a long way to helping Samuel feel more comfortable about the prospect of the flights. The demonstration also showed us we would need to figure how to support his head during the transfer process, valuable information that we could use to move forward in planning. It was a very worthwhile visit.

To get Samuel to Canberra we needed to consider all the elements involved in boarding and disembarking the aeroplane, as well as his comfort and safety during the flight itself. Together with the handling team, we worked out plans for:

- Hoisting Samuel inside the aircraft cabin, strapping him into his aisle seat.
- Positioning the ventilator, the suction unit and emergency equipment within arm's reach (under the seat in front). These needed to be secured in accordance with transport regulations, but at the same time be fully accessible.
- Dismantling his power chair so it would fit in the cargo hold. On the day, I followed a well-practised procedure to do this in under ten minutes on the air bridge.
- How cabin pressure would affect ventilator settings and whether adjustments would be needed.
- Emergency evacuation from the aircraft...

The support from Qantas, both in pre-planning and on the flight, was second to none. The aircraft had already been delayed into Brisbane and the time it took us to load quite likely delayed its departure even further. From our seats, Amelia and I breathed a sigh of relief when we saw the cargo carrier outside the aircraft bring Samuel's wheelchair to the cargo hatch only to draw a slight gasp as moments later, we saw it reverse away from the plane with the wheelchair still on it. Handlers eventually managed to load it on to one of the cargo-loading conveyors and into the hold below us. On board, the flight attendants made us feel at ease—in their eyes, before anyone else was allowed into the cabin, we were their only clients. They were concerned for our welfare as well as Samuel's, making sure Samuel and his vital equipment were safely secured. They ensured we were well hydrated and nourished during the flight and took a genuine interest in our story.

Of course, the flight was just one element of the trip. There were many other Plan Bs and Cs to be considered, and problems to be solved along the way. If we couldn't fix an issue as it arose, we worked around it as best we could, but made a note of it so that we could give it further consideration at a later date, with the aim of making future trips easier.

And then, there was packing. For Samuel's week in Canberra, we needed to bring:

- Emergency tracheostomy kit with spare tracheostomy tubes, scissors and chain cutters. Getting these through security at the airport was an interesting challenge.
- Backup ventilator and spare (third) ventilator.
- Enough 'wet' and 'dry' circuits and filters to last the week. ('Wet' ventilator circuits are used at night and have moisture added to the ventilator air supply from a humidifier.)
- Humidifier and water bags for the humidifier.
- Suction units, manual back-up suction units and suction catheters.
- Resuscitation (resus) bag. Used as the last backup if all ventilators fail and to assist with removing lung secretions.
- Shower chair and other toileting equipment.
- Night-time ventilator stand.
- Feed, feed lines and feed pump.
- Chargers (for everything), extension cords and power boards.
- Portable hoist, slings, clamps, syringes.
- House bricks to raise the height of the bed to keep it higher than the water-filled humidifier. If the levels aren't right, water will flow through the ventilator circuit directly into Samuel's lungs.
- And of course, Samuel's very heavy power chair.

Gone are our days of travelling light. This is the list of things we now need for pretty much *any* trip, whether it's a single night away or a two-week holiday. The sheer amount of planning and equipment involved means it rarely makes sense to have fewer than four or five nights away—especially given the effort it takes to set everything up at our destination, and then pack up again to come home.

Last but not least, we also needed to arrange for support worker/s to assist us in Canberra so that all the family could get some sleep at night. Jane sourced a nurse through an agency in Canberra to do the night shifts for us and Amelia came along too, as our extra night-time backup. It may have been Samuel's school trip, but its success was a whole-family effort and we hoped it would be a memorable trip for all of us.

The night nurse turned out to have a good sense of humour to go with her thick Irish accent, and Samuel took great delight in asking her questions like 'What is 11 x 3?', just to hear her say 'tirty-tree', and calling out 'Nurse, I need a trache suction, I need a trache suction, I need a trache suction! Come on, I've asked *ye tree times*!'

We had two ground-floor units in the motel where Samuel's classmates were staying. Amelia and Samuel slept in one with the nurse watching over the equipment while Jane and I took the other. In the evenings, after bathroom routines were completed, a couple of his friends were allowed to come to Samuel's room for a while to hang out and maybe watch a bit of TV. Samuel conducted drive-pasts of their rooms in his power chair, and where space allowed, he could even join them for a quick chat.

By day, most of the trip went according to plan. Samuel was able to join the class for most of their activities, and I was on cloud nine to think all our efforts had paid off.

But at the Australian War Memorial, of all places, our careful planning came undone.

The elevator to the Shrine of Remembrance, the most sacred place in the memorial, would not accommodate Samuel's chair. Neither Samuel nor I had strength left in our collective problem-solving tanks to fix this one. We were spent.

On previous trips to Canberra, I had found the shrine to be a truly special place. Spending time there is an opportunity to reflect on all that is important about life in Australia—and it was an experience I desperately wanted to share with Samuel. As I've said, it is my belief that this country is made great by the strength of the Australian Constitution—a constitution that has been defended by the many men and women whose memory is honoured in the shrine. And it is the constitution that has given us the standard of health care without which Samuel would not have survived.

A visit to the War Memorial is a deeply moving experience at any time, but on this occasion, I could not contain my sadness. After all our efforts, Samuel couldn't make it to this special place. Samuel took the disappointment in his stride, attempting to downplay any fuss he may have thought I was about to create. But I took it as a personal moment of defeat. I had set this as my goal for Samuel to be able to experience given all he had been through in the last nineteen months. Between the main entrance and the Pool of Reflection I stood, tears streaming down my face, inconsolable and shattered.

Overall, though, the Canberra Tour was a success. Samuel has very fond memories of the trip, which is, after all, what we had hoped. Despite the complex travel arrangements, the difficulties of hoisting Samuel in the aisle of the 737, the discomforts of the flight, and even the need to use the resuscitation bag mid-flight in view of other passengers, we made it to and from the freezing cold capital in July 2017. Samuel was able to join his mates for this traditional rite of passage and to feel like he was one of them. And we were able to show him that while many doors were closed to him, with planning and perseverance, it was possible to force others open—and keep them that way.

Samuel could fly. And just like the superhero decal atop his 10th birthday cake, Samuel, too, was a Superman.

## In Summary–planning:

- Strategically planning for a future based on current conditions does not mean hope is being abandoned.
- Set some goals for the short, medium or longer term. It's better to have a starting point than nothing at all.
- If you think you will have ongoing high-level needs, consider what entity might best support you.

- If you see even half an opportunity to advocate or make fruitful connections, trust your instincts, be brave and take the plunge. You have nothing to lose, everything to gain and you won't die wondering. Fortune really favours the brave.

- Ask the hospital teams for advice. They will have a good idea of what equipment and supplies you will need. They can help you to sort this into 'must haves', 'should haves' and 'could haves'. Then aim to get all of them.

- Ask your rehab team to step in when benefactors offer to buy items of equipment. Yes, we need a hoist, but I am time-poor and don't understand all the specifications it needs to meet.

- If you are eligible for the NDIS, don't presume it will cover everything you need. Remember the key phrases: 'Choice and Control' and 'Reasonable and Necessary'—these permeate everything to do with the NDIS.

- There is no better time to harness the financial goodwill of the community than when your story enters the public domain. If you have control over when you go public, plan for it as best as you can. If not, run with it as hard and fast and as long as you possibly can. Milk every moment for what it's worth. It may be your only opportunity.

- Capitalise on the capabilities of immediate family and friends. We found it hard to ask, but often they want to help—they just need to know what is required.

- Sometimes asking an expert is best, and it can help take egos and personalities out of the equation. If you risk offending Uncle Mark or cousin Ethel by not taking them up on an offer of help—even though you think they aren't well-suited to the task—being able to explain your decision-making process can defuse the situation.

- It can be really hard to ask for 'handouts', but you may find others are happy to do this on your behalf.

- Don't try to micro-manage fundraising. While it's important to keep an eye out for fraudsters, allow people you trust to have some latitude. Their motives are to support you.
- Here are some of the fundraising activities other people organised in support of Samuel:
  - A charity Zumba session
  - Barbeque stall at Markets on Grand
  - Coffee Club tipping jars
  - Meadowbrook IGA collection tins
  - Trivia Night and Auction
  - Raffles
  - School, free-dress days
  - Linen parties
  - Sausage sizzles
  - Garden party
  - High tea
  - Shave for Samuel and Crazy Hair Day

El Camino: Samuel's Poppy, Eric, at 83 years young, raised awareness and funds with his third walk of the Camino Frances. He walked from St Jean Pied du Port in France, over the Pyrenees, eventually reaching Santiago de Compostela where he obtained his Compostela—the certificate of completion—endorsed with Samuel's name. Jane's brother, Simeon, also trekked the Camino in 2017 in honour of Samuel.

# Practicalities

## Work

When Samuel first became ill, I was fortunate to have plenty of long-service and sick leave I could use. It was one less thing to worry about. But as it became clear that Samuel was going to be in hospital for many months, we started to consider our options. Jane and I figured that I could scrape through most of 2016 using up all my leave if I had to, but that would leave nothing in reserve for later if we needed it. The best option would be for me to return to work, if at all possible, to keep time up our sleeve for whatever rainy days lay ahead.

I wasn't ready to return to my school. My emotions were still raw, and I feared that I wouldn't cope well with the day-to-day problem-solving required, the issues and disagreements that are a deputy principal's daily bread. The families at my school were very supportive of staff but I was worried about my own capacity to function appropriately. If a parent were to come to me with a trivial complaint—say, a child's broken lunchbox—I couldn't be confident that I would have handled it in the professional manner expected.

Luckily, some of my close colleagues were talking with someone, who was talking with someone else.

I was offered a gig in the Education Department's Mt Gravatt Regional Office, and I remain forever grateful to those who made this possible. It was ideal. Jane could drop me to work in the morning en route to the hospital. In the afternoon, I could catch a bus to the hospital to see Samuel and help with his evening routine, then travel home with Jane at night. And thankfully, it meant I was never in a position where I might be tempted to tell someone just what they could do with their broken lunchbox.

A significant and early part of the job was data tracking with spreadsheets. Good friends, knowing about my inner geek, had once made me a magnet with the words 'Keep Calm... and make an Excel spreadsheet'. This was stuff I could do easily and without needing to be overly strategic—a skill required in my usual leadership role. I could immerse myself in the task and feel I had genuinely contributed to the work that needed doing. And I felt I was good at it.

My new colleagues didn't know about my situation, and this suited me, especially at first. I didn't want to blurt out my story. I kept my new workplace separate from my personal life, consciously choosing not to impose my grief on others. And truthfully, I don't think I could have handled any more of the sorts of expressions of shock and sympathy that Samuel's story usually elicited from new acquaintances. I simply needed to build my own work credibility. Without this, I felt I would have become a function of our horrible situation—beholden to it forever. My new boss introduced me to the team, saying I would be working on a 'little project' for her. This, as I learnt later, was her discreet way of saying, 'Yes, there is a story behind this but don't ask me now—I'm not going to tell you why, but I'm helping this person for good reason.' Thanks, Boss!

For a while, I hated Mondays. Actually, Monday afternoons.

Back at work after the weekend, I felt distanced from the reality of Samuel's plight. I wasn't dealing well with the continuous parade of therapists and consultants, but in the office, I had genuine respite.

Naturally, I felt guilty. After all, Jane and Samuel were still dealing with everything back at the hospital and here I was enjoying the relative ease of my paid work. In my head, I knew the shared daily parenting routine we'd nurtured during the first few months in hospital was not sustainable. At some point, we needed to settle into the roles we were more likely to follow into the future. This assuaged my guilt a little.

But the truth was, heading to the office felt like stepping back into our old life—going to work each day, just as I had in the years 'before'.

Stepping out of the elevator to head back to the hospital each afternoon was an entirely different story. On the 800-metre walk to the bus, the grief, the anguish, the anger, the 'everything' came flooding back in. The wailing that followed was sometimes so loud, it's a wonder it didn't cause a traffic incident, with drivers looking around to see where the siren was coming from. Crying in public felt intense, yet weirdly private. As much as I hated my powerlessness to stop the tears, in hindsight I was grateful—they were a pressure-release valve. By the time I got to the hospital I had regained my composure and was ready to tackle whatever the evening held. And by Friday, after a week in the office, my emotions felt better regulated and under my control.

I am grateful for the many genuine work friends I made in the Mount Gravatt office. They did eventually become aware of my background after our story went public in May 2016. And all were supportive, to the point they'd even take the mickey out of me at any opportunity, making me feel even more like one of the crew. Treated normally—which was just what I needed. Way to go team!

## What I Learned: Getting Back to Work

- Avail yourself of any industrial or other entitlements you can. They are there for a reason.
- If you find yourself in a position to get back to work in some way, do so. Throw your mind and heart into it as much as you can.
- Be mindful of your colleagues' capacity to offer support. Don't be a drain on their emotions by presuming you are the only person with issues.

- Bosses: knowing what supportive return-to-work pathways are available is really useful, especially if you can think outside the box. The staff who work more closely with the colleague needing support may well be the best-placed to know their needs. Give them jobs you know they can manage, even if they aren't the high-yield tasks you would normally expect of them.

- While you're at work, concentrating on practical tasks, the difficulties of your private life may recede—only to come flooding back at the end of the day. If possible, try to take a bit of time—even a few minutes—to release pent-up emotions before you step back into the family environment.

## Education

Given her age and maturity, it was easy for us to think that Amelia was doing just fine. After all, she had just successfully completed a Griffith University subject during grade 12, which guaranteed her entry to her chosen course, midwifery. She also topped this off with a Sir Samuel Griffith Scholarship.

But at a time when she seemed poised to soar, she stumbled and seemed to struggle with the transition to the more adult world of university. The details of her struggles are not mine to share, but suffice to say, it became blindingly apparent to us that, as parents, we had taken our eye off the ball at a critical point in her life. Because Amelia's response to the harrowing twists and turns of Samuel's illness had been so measured and mature, we had forgotten that in some ways she was still a young person needing support.

Would we have made the same mistakes if she'd been closer in age to Samuel? Of if she'd been younger, more obviously in need of 'parenting'?

I don't have any answers for this. But with the benefit of hindsight, I can only stress how crucial it is for parents in situations like ours to do their utmost to support the siblings of the sick child.

Samuel's own return to school was measured, meticulously planned and incredibly important—a major focus of his reintegration into regular life pursuits. As a teacher, I've experienced firsthand the rich tapestry of simple and complex social relationships between growing children that a conventional school-based education provides. Until his illness, Samuel had been a child who thrived in the school environment, and we believed it was important for his state of mind that he be able to return to that environment.

Samuel's doctors were keen to do all they could to facilitate ways that he could connect with his classmates at Springwood Road State School. A keen paediatrician (the one with the laminated, foot-signed periodic table in his home study) even investigated whether it might be possible to set up a telepresence robot, a type of tablet or smartphone-controlled device that could have allowed Samuel to have a sort of virtual presence in the school, and to interact with his teachers and peers. At the time, the idea didn't prove practical, but it highlighted the value Samuel's doctors placed on the continuity of his education. In the meantime, the hospital school's bedside lessons established a routine of expectations, and his teachers sought ways to tap into his interests. They successfully built on what he could do—including, as already mentioned, his artistic talents.

Staff at Springwood Road were also finding ways for him to connect with the school. The principal and other key staff worked together to set up regular Thursday visits to the hospital by various teachers, teacher aides and students. Obviously, this was wonderful for Samuel, but it also enabled his classmates to develop an understanding of his situation, making his eventual return to school easier—less awkward and strange for both him and them. By the time he returned, everyone there knew about his condition and seemed comfortable around him, treating him normally. Interestingly, the transition to high school and a new cohort of students who were unfamiliar with Samuel's story, proved more challenging and resulted, at first, in him feeling disconnected from his peers and his studies.

We remain grateful to Samuel's teachers for their complete dedication to making education accessible for him, and for showing him that although so much of his life had changed, he could still be an active participant in school life and that he could succeed—that he still had plenty to give.

A great many people were involved in managing and supporting Samuel's return to school, and many obstacles needed to be overcome.

As teachers ourselves, Jane and I naturally wanted to be involved in the transition planning. In my job, I'd worked in the area of inclusion for students with disabilities. Although I realised our primary role as parents was to advocate for Samuel's needs, I sometimes found it hard not to be judgemental when some school staff didn't seem to fully grasp the fundamental principles of inclusion.

In an education context, these principles are about reasonable adjustments to support access to the curriculum. Along with other elements, they need to be embedded in a culture of genuine acceptance that 'persons with a disability have the same fundamental rights as the rest of the community.' The Commonwealth Disability Discrimination Act (1992) sets out these principles.

The Act also addresses 'unjustifiable hardship', in that those who need to make reasonable adjustments may be released from that obligation if doing so would impose an unjustifiable hardship upon them. But I would contend that in Australia, no government (including their respective departments and agencies) could reasonably argue that they would be suffering unjustifiable hardship in the provision of funding to support Samuel's access to education.

The Act has been in place for as long as I have been married, but it has taken many years for it to be widely adopted and accepted as fundamentally commonplace. I think it is fair to say, its application remains patchy even now.

In hindsight, I probably didn't give the school the best chance to shine as it grappled with its obligations. At the time, I still found it difficult to trust that other people had the ability to take all of Samuel's needs into account when planning opportunities for him. Fortunately, the staff proved willing to work with us in most areas of planning. Certainly, they recognised I was well-versed in how the school's Canberra Tour operated and that I was well-positioned to complement their efforts to ensure Samuel's part in the trip was a success.

## What I learned: Getting Back to Education

- Don't forget your other children—and their education.
- During a lengthy hospital stay, continuing your child's education is critical. Maintaining social and educational links with their school can be a crucial element on their path to recovery.
- Encourage visits between school and hospital. Don't discount the possibility of telepresence robots—the Queensland Children's Hospital School will have some advice on this.
- Monitor the coordination of the back-to-school transition, but don't be too quick to intervene. Institutions need to own their part of the process.
- Advocate! Don't allow excuses to be made for not accommodating your child's needs, but don't bludgeon the school (or anyone) with your knowledge of the Disability Discrimination Act. Understand that for high-level cases like Samuel's, there will be significant training and resourcing demands on the school. Inclusion doesn't start with the checklists and planning; it starts in your mind and it starts in your heart.
- Making it happen will be a team effort.
- If a child will be returning to school with a lot of medical equipment, other students—particularly younger children—will benefit from an explanation about what all of the devices are and what the child's needs are. Making everyone comfortable with the situation helps break down barriers and promotes true inclusion.

## Back Home

Although the Canberra Tour was a major goal for us, our biggest priority from late 2016 was getting Samuel home. No parent likes to see their child in hospital, still less for an extended period, so it came as a bit of a surprise to realise the extent to which we had become institutionalised, lulled by the sense of safety that being in the PICU environment provided. When you spend a long time in hospital—whether as patient or parent—

it is easy to become so comfortable with its familiar daily routines that you lose sight of normal life. And when the 'new normal' awaiting you outside the hospital is likely to hold so many challenges, is it any wonder the prospect of leaving hospital is daunting? But that time was fast approaching. After 16 months, we were tired. Samuel was medically stable and well. We wanted to take him home.

Discharging Samuel was never going to be straightforward. By now we had a pretty good idea of how life at home would work, but before we agreed to his discharge, we needed to make sure everything was ready for him.

There were three main areas of activity: we were overseeing the modifications needed to make our home suitable for Samuel's needs; CHQ at Home was overseeing the recruitment and training of support workers; and the hospital rehab team was busy carrying out trials of the equipment that would be coming home with us. Each group was often keen to learn the progress of the other, partly to coordinate, but certainly for our part, we didn't want to be responsible for delaying discharge.

With some difficulty, Jane and I were able to balance our busy schedules to share the load of overseeing details of the house modifications work. I was liaising with the builder, Jane was coordinating with the rehab team, and we collaborated as and when we could.

As an added complication, CHQ at Home was bidding against Mater at Home to take on the 'Hospital in the Home' program (which included the Home Ventilation program) through the Department of Health. Until the tender process was completed, the recruitment of new support workers—to complement those who came across from the Mater at Home program—was on hold. But CHQ staff were trying hard to get this done.

The rehab team was working at top speed to complete the equipment trials. But 'top speed' in this realm, through no fault of the rehab team's, felt like a snail's pace. Companies needed to be booked to bring their products to the ward for Samuel to try, because he couldn't go to them.

Sometimes, frustratingly, there were cancellations, but nevertheless most trials progressed well enough for the team to agree on a suitable bed, as well as wheelchairs (powered and manual), a mobile hoist and sling. Seeing the painstaking care and thought that went into testing and selecting each item of equipment so that it best accommodated Samuel's particular needs was an education.

The shower chair, seemingly such a simple thing, was a particular stumbling block. Our occupational therapist was at her wits' end. After many weeks and test-driving what seemed like fifty commodes—although it was probably only four or five—one was found that was deemed satisfactory. It was just as well—there were no others left to try. Where the others had been hard and unforgiving, this Goldilocks chair had a flexible, soft vinyl backrest, better suited to supporting his torso with its early signs of a twisting and hunching scoliosis—a condition that many people with spinal cord injury must face.

Where possible, we tried to include Samuel in decisions surrounding the home modifications. (We preferred not to call them 'renovations', a term that implied we had simply chosen to embark on home improvements). The work would take months, and we discussed with him whether it might be better to move into a sort of halfway house for a while, or stay in hospital until he could return to the only home he had even known. Like us, he preferred to make the move in one step—a clean break from hospital life. Spending a few months in modified accommodation might have given us a feel for how to optimise the positioning of equipment, power points, services, bathroom layouts and so on in our own home, but it would also have meant a lot of additional planning. Given how much time and energy we were already spending on getting Samuel home, it was too much to contemplate. We put the idea aside.

Other decisions, like what 'stuff' we needed to cull at home, were made for us by a twist of fate.

In May 2016, while we were—as usual—at the hospital, a pipe in our ensuite bathroom burst. A call from our security company alerted us to the fact that the power had gone out at home, and returning from the city, we discovered that 11,000 litres of water had inundated the entire house. Many things were beyond salvaging, which at least made it simple to decide what to do with them.

Almost everything else needed to be removed and stored for future use, or else given away, or sold. We knew we needed to declutter, to create a more open living space that Samuel could easily navigate in his wheelchair, but we couldn't do this without his input and acceptance. Each decision about whether to keep a toy or donate it to charity involved emotion-laden deliberations. The acceptance of the loss for Samuel, in giving up his favourite belongings, was perhaps assuaged by a hope that his disability may yet prove temporary, and that most things could be replaced.

Through connections at our swimming club, the Rochedale Rays, we were introduced to Barney at BMR Building Services who agreed to take on the home modifications. Were it not for this introduction, we would not have known who to trust. We owe an endless debt of gratitude to Barney for reaching out to us (and to his wife, who may have whispered the idea in his ear), and to Rob for taking on the role of project manager. Between them, they called in any number of favours and worked with their sub-contractors to keep costs as low as possible.

Behind the scenes, Rob had the tricky finance conversations with other people on our behalf.

There was no shortage of tradespeople offering to help, and while most offers were genuine, not all were alike in usefulness and altruism. The best offers were those that aimed to get the best job done at the best price, as soon as possible. Others promised to get the job done quickly, but were vague about the cost—'don't worry about the money now'—which implied the possibility of a dirty big invoice at the end. Thanks to Rob and others, we were largely shielded from having to sort out which offers were worth accepting. Our supporters also learnt quickly to clarify offers of help from tradies by asking blunt questions about money on our behalf. With so many offers coming our way, it would have been easy for us not to have seen the dodgy ones—we didn't have the emotional energy to be anything other than trusting.

Once Rob had a good picture of what was needed, we found we could leave him to deal with many of the hundreds of decisions that had to be made. And when our input was needed—for choosing tiles or working out the kitchen design, for instance—Rob sourced the suppliers and talked to them ahead of time, to try to ensure they had a few well-considered options ready for us to choose between. We didn't have time for lengthy comparisons of every different material or colour of bathroom tile, or to weigh up the pros and cons of different countertops. We needed to trust people. I reckon the kitchen we ended up with is the best we've ever had, and instead of taking months to decide on benchtops, layouts and tiles, with expert guidance, we had everything chosen in under half an hour.

Inevitably, some decisions weren't as functionally perfect as we would have liked, but we needed to let some things go through to the keeper. Sometimes, because of all the other discharge planning and training happening at hospital, Jane and I simply couldn't be in the same place at the same time to make a joint decision.

We agreed to live with whatever decisions the other made—knowing that most things could be 'fixed' at some point in the future when life was less stressful. One good tip, though, for anyone who finds themselves in a similar situation to ours: If your house modifications involve electrical work, check with the hospital to see if they need to have someone review your plans. Medical equipment needs particular consideration with regards to electrics, and all of our work was done before we were advised of this. Thankfully, after hospital technicians spoke with our builder and his electricians about the wiring and the circuit loads, it was determined that none of our work needing redoing.

The following is a brief timeline of the work that got underway in December 2016:

- Temporary ramp installed at rear of house for Samuel to be able to visit and monitor progress as permitted. It was critical he felt connected to the project.
- Side pathway redone for temporary wheelchair access to the ramp.
- Demolition of carport walls (under main roof area of house) and removal of roller door.
- Slab poured in carport, level with main house slab.
- Carport enclosed to make Amelia's new bedroom.
- House window removed; window cavity enlarged to become Amelia's bedroom door.
- Front garden razed and levelled.
- Six-metre shipping container placed in front yard.
- During summer vacation, house emptied of belongings and stored in shipping container.
- Early 2017, Amelia, Jane and I moved into accommodation at Kangaroo Point near the 'Gabba. (This, incredibly, was close enough to hear Adele's two Brisbane concerts and warm-up sessions as clear as day—the best two concerts we've never been to!)
- Main living area internal walls demolished.
- Internal walls and wardrobes separating Samuel and Amelia's original bedrooms demolished to make a single bigger bedroom for Samuel.
- Bathroom and toilet walls demolished.
- Kitchen fitted out.
- Samuel's room finished with ceiling hoist track.
- Bathroom and living area finished, painted/tiled.
- Floor coverings.
- Shipping container emptied of most belongings. A two-day garage sale disposed of whatever we'd decided we no longer needed.
- Temporary timber ramp installed at the newly-widened front door.

By March 2017, the house was finished enough that it could receive Samuel. We had a full roster of trained support workers. We were ready.

Getting out of the hospital on discharge day had been a big enough affair—with images of Samuel cast on the big screens in the hospital foyer, and the way to the exit lined with staff who'd been able to answer the call from the CEO Fionnagh Dougan and form a clapping, cheering guard of honour—but we'd opted not to invite the media. We were very aware that if something critical didn't work once we got home, we would need to turn around and go back to hospital. Fortunately, the morning went without a hiccup. We also chose not to have a CHQ at Home support worker join us until the afternoon—which meant we had a few treasured hours alone at home as a family.

For the first time in 480 nights, we were all sleeping under the same roof. Yes, a support worker arrived for the afternoon shift, but at least, we were all together again.

Home at last.

## What I learned: Getting Back Home

- Long-stay admissions can become strangely comfortable, especially if the prospect of life after discharge is daunting, so it's important to remain focussed on the goal of getting home.
- Involve your child in the decision-making process, and try to arrange site visits during modification work if they seem interested. Do they want to see changes as they happen, or just the final product?
- Be in control of discharge planning: ensuring your home is as ready as possible before discharge will make the start of your post-hospital life smoother.
- Using a project manager for building work will free you up for all the other planning tasks that will require your attention.
- Seek clarity about offers of help from tradespeople—are they genuinely offering you the best deal? Or might they send you a hefty invoice later?

- Aside from the NDIS, you may be able to access other one-off disability support funds to finance specific modifications. For example, to pay for a house ramp or bathroom access.

- Decisions, decisions! There will be hundreds of them. A good project manager can ease this burden. If a decision turns out to be less than perfect, try to see it as a bridge to cross further down the track—something to think about when you have less to do. In this way, 'wrong decisions' can become 'new opportunities'.

- Will the discharge from hospital be a media affair? Or is your priority just to get home? If you're unsure, trust your instincts. Keeping it as a private family occasion was right for us.

- Take a moment to savour the fact that you are all together again, as you should be. You made it!

# Part 3—The Futures

# Paying it Forward

## Our Challenge

Jane and I have always tried to 'do our bit' for the community. Over the years, we've turned snags at fundraisers for P&Cs, sold raffle tickets for swimming club, baked cakes for netball and supervised stalls at more school fairs than I can recall. Between us, we've pretty much held every different committee role in these groups over the years. I think we've always tried to hold true to the moral imperative that if you have the capacity to help others, you should. There's a certain amount of satisfaction that comes from knowing that we have done our small part to make this place a better world, and that we have contributed to our local 'economy' of emotional and social support.

This community engagement was one of the first casualties when Samuel fell ill. Clearly, we would not be in a position to contribute to the greater good for a long time. 'The greater good', for us, became limited to precisely whatever Samuel needed, a situation that has continued. Before we are in a position to contribute, we must first accomplish the day-to-day stuff that is routine but essential. With me back in fulltime work, it is Jane who manages the support-worker roster, tracks the equipment maintenance schedule and feed regimes, orders the special liquid feed for Samuel and the water for his humidifier, as well as organising the next pharmacy or supplies order from the hospital. It is relentless—a fulltime job.

Then there are the extra tasks—a wheelchair service to be arranged, a problem with the bed to be sorted, Samuel's portable eye-gaze computer needs a program loaded for school. It goes on.

Nonetheless, we are determined to be able to pay it forward (or back) in some way. We want to give back to those who have helped, and to those who need help. And gradually, we hope to reconsolidate our own sense of worth.

## Casual Support

We find ourselves paying it forward in casual, unplanned ways. Sometimes it is just offering an understanding ear to families with children in PICU, listening to the depth of pain and despair of people who walk a similar path to ours. Sometimes we share our experiences of dealing with the NDIS with fellow members of the boccia club where Samuel is now a regular player, offering tips on strategy and funding.

In its simplest form, this might mean suggesting they include broad goals in their NDIS plan that focus on their community participation and engagement. We might suggest they include examples in the client narrative at the front of their plan to highlight how funding for specific needs would contribute to the achievement of these goals. NDIS planners are under extreme pressure to minimise expenses, so making it easy for them to understand the details of a client's needs can help them justify funding to their managers.

## Conferences & Presentations

I like to think that the lessons we've learned along the way, the insights we've had—and the mistakes we've made—might be useful for other families to know, as well as for the hospital and educational staff who have the power to make positive impacts.

Our 480 days in PICU gave us a little bit of credibility with the hospital and I have never had a sense that our feedback wasn't valued. Partly, I think this is because we have always tried to provide it in a positive way.

One area of particular interest to me has been the Individual Health Management Plans that state schools use to assist staff in supporting students with significant and/or chronic health needs: severe asthma, anaphylaxis, renal complications etc. Framed in terms of clinical presentation, general management, critical management/treatments and outlining the responsibilities for staff and families, these plans provide a basis for managing inherent risk—the likelihood of an incident against its potential severity. Their purpose is to keep children as safe as possible while they are learning at school. Needless to say, Samuel's plan is very detailed. Because of the preventative and protective measures in place, the likelihood of an incident is very slim—but the outcome could be severe and easily fatal.

These plans have had to be tweaked and rethought as Samuel has grown. His early plans required two trache/vent-trained staff to be no more than five metres away from him at all times. As he grew older, this drove him nuts and we needed to increase the distance, as uncomfortable as it was for his support staff. Samuel needed his space—without that, we knew his state of mind would be at risk. And as detailed as his school health plans were, they didn't address the issue of Samuel's mental health.

It seemed like an obvious oversight to me.

I took the opportunity to tackle the issue in a presentation for a Therapists Nurses Teachers conference in 2018, arranged by the State Schools Nursing Service. I argued that mental health is a valid consideration when mitigating risk for students with health plans. I included some confronting statistics out of the United States showing the high rates of depression and suicide among people living with transverse myelitis: suicide is the leading cause of death among sufferers, accounting for more than half of all deaths.

Since then, I have discovered the Department of Education is planning to modify its health plan templates to include a section on maintaining student welfare, which can include mental health considerations. Although I have no way of knowing whether my contribution directly influenced this change, I am pleased it is happening. And it would be nice to think that lessons learned from Samuel's health plan experiences have led in some small way to better support systems for other school children.

## Matrix of Support

I also spoke at the Hospital Educators Learners Parents (H.E.L.P.) Conference in 2019, presenting an outline for how hospital and education staff can help minimise the stress on a patient's family. It is a model that can be applied by health or education staff to guide supporters and well-wishers into offering families like ours the right type of support at the right time. Fundamentally, it encompasses support that ranges in nature from the emotional end of the spectrum to the purely practical and addresses the issue of how to offer the right support at the right time. Plotted against each other, these make up what I have called the Matrix of Support, first mentioned in section 2. In my presentation, I also outlined what the different types of support may look like across the four quadrants.

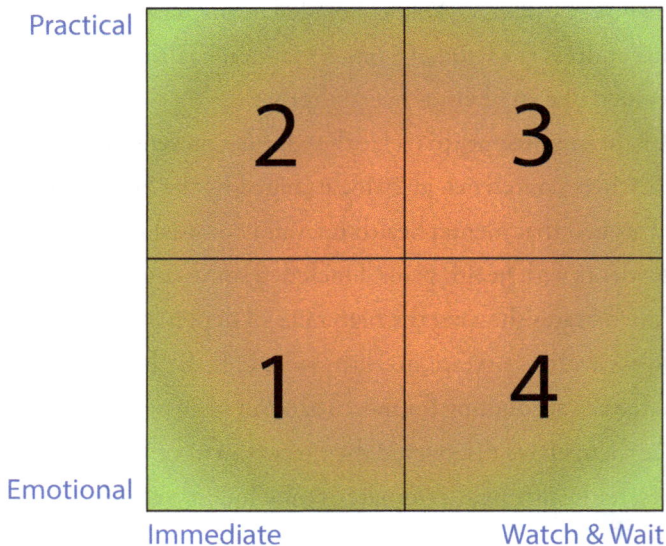

*The Matrix of Support plots the two dimensions of the nature of support (Emotional and Practical) against the timeliness of the support being offered.*

- Quadrant 1: Typically, will involve people very close to the family; patience; empathy; individual coping; makes sure the family's immediate personal/emotional needs are taken care of.
- Quadrant 2: Problem-solving focus; basic necessities; food; parking costs; involving others to take action.
- Quadrant 3: Futures oriented; long-term life solutions; motivating others to support and take action.
- Quadrant 4: Patience; empathy; concern for the fabric of the family/marriage/relationships.

The model was born out of my observations of people's behaviour during the 16 months Samuel was in hospital. It links closely to another concept I've called the Continuum of Functional Capacity.

## Continuum of Functional Capacity

This continuum came from my reflections on my own capacity during Samuel's admission. The components making up such a continuum may vary from person to person, but I chose to label them Coping, Comprehending and Proactivity. Given my love of spreadsheets and statistics, it perhaps comes as little surprise that framing this model as a graph helped me to understand the ways my ability to 'function'—to cope, to comprehend and to be proactive— fluctuated over the sixteen months. It also made me wonder how other parents in similar situations navigate their own continua. Might the parents of a child admitted for an emergency appendectomy experience similar functional ups and downs, condensed into the few days of the hospital stay? Even though the functional dynamics of their crisis experience may be compressed compared to mine, I believe they still exist and will have an impact on the level and type of support they need.

Looking back over our family's journey from Part 1 of this book, I can overlay some key features of my own functional capacity, beginning in the emergency department on Day 1 and ending with Samuel's discharge sixteen months later:

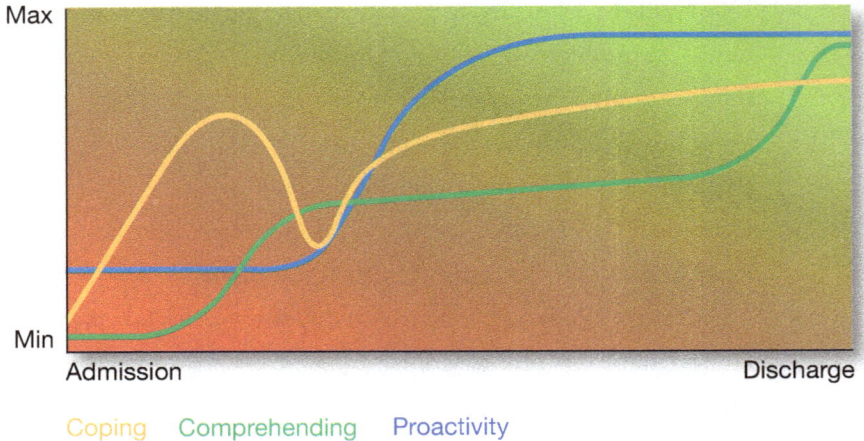

Coping     Comprehending     Proactivity

*The graphic shows the contrasting elements across the sixteen months of admission. The dip in the 'coping' line was at the time of the worst bad news during May 2016. Very shortly after this turning point, we really began to understand the gravity of the situation and strengthened in our resolve to empower ourselves.*

- COPING: My coping levels were initially low. They steadily increased as the days went on, dropping off significantly immediately following 'bad news' days, then increasing again as I reluctantly accepted the gravity of Samuel's prognosis.

- COMPREHENDING: My comprehension levels were low to begin with, when we really didn't understand much of what was happening, and there was a steep learning curve early on. Then, although my coping levels dipped, my comprehension steadily increased throughout Samuel's stay, with a significant jump closer to the discharge date, as we came to grips with the knowledge and training required to support him at home.

- PROACTIVITY: Always steady and consistent in our efforts to support Samuel, our 'proactivity' levels jumped markedly once we resolved that it would take a high level of commitment and dedication from us to reach discharge and move forward in life.

Of course, adding elements like financial security, physical wellbeing and spirituality to the mix would provide a fuller picture of the complexity of this model of functional capacity. But by attempting to plot just a few of mine, I hope I have given readers some idea of the functional dynamics that may be in play when a loved one is admitted to hospital. I am also not suggesting that readers immediately start graphing where they or their loved ones may be as they progress through their issues. It is suffice to recognise that there will be different ups and downs at play for everyone involved.

## Linking the Matrix and Continuum

This knowledge can guide family, friends and other supporters as they try to work out what measures of assistance best suit the needs of the patient's parents at particular points.

During Samuel's admission, I observed that people have a comfort zone within which they feel most useful, most able to help a family or person in crisis. It may be as an immediate or early responder, or they may 'watch and wait' to see what is needed. And the type of support ranges between emotional and practical. Too many offers of practical help may not be what's best for a family in the early stages of a crisis, while emotional support may be less needed later on when the family is grappling with the practicalities of day-to-day life. Everyone can have a role to play, but by recognising what support you are best suited to provide—and when the best time is to step forward—you can ease the pressure a family is under. This also makes it easier for the family to accept and manage the generosity of others.

If parents are cognitively overloaded—still struggling to process new and difficult information—then expecting them to make other practical decisions (in our case, for instance, about fundraising or future house modifications) can be extremely stressful.

Similarly, once they reach a point where they are coping well, comprehending and being highly proactive, then frequent offers of emotional support (constant hugging, sitting talking for hours at a time) may be less helpful, and may actually become a source of stress.

While it would not be appropriate for health or education staff to intervene or prevent authentic offers of support, their knowledge and experience means they may be well placed to direct would-be helpers with suggestions for what sort of support is most useful, and when.

This is a deliberately simplified explanation: the support dynamic is inherently more complex in real life. But I hope that by breaking it down like this, someone, somewhere, will be able to apply my ideas to ease the pressures of a family in crisis.

In our case, the more proactive and empowered we became, the better placed we were to graciously accept offers of practical support. And our sense of empowerment grew, at least in part, *because* of the practical support that poured in during the early days—measures like the meals roster and donations to pay for hospital parking fees. To all community members, friends and family who supported us at the right time in just the right way—thank you!

## Support for the Children's Hospital

Even Samuel has embraced opportunities to 'give back' to the people and institutions that provided him with care and support. Each May, the Queensland Children's Hospital hosts an assessment process for physicians wishing to be admitted to the Royal Australian College of Paediatricians. They require a number of case studies. Volunteer 'patients' are first assessed by an experienced consultant, and then examined by the candidate physician, who must then immediately report on their findings to the senior consultants tasked with determining the candidate's proficiency. Samuel happily offers his services as a 'patient', often making the consultants (who generally haven't met him) aware of his advanced sense of humour. I like to hope that the candidates report on the patient's sense of humour as part of their examination. After all, sometimes that humour is all that gets young people and their families from one day to the next.

An invitation from the hospital's CEO, Fionnagh Dougan, to speak at the launch of the hospital's new mission statement with its vision and values, was my first opportunity to share publicly our family's situation. Asked to speak about the value of 'care', I chose to place it within the context of 'The Journey'—not just our family's lengthy journey, but also the care that is evident even in more common, short-stay admissions. I tried to cover as many of the ways in which this care is manifested in the efforts of staff, and concluded with the importance of staff caring for each other. For an edited version of my presentation, you can go to www.childrens.health.qld.gov.au/chq/ about-us/our-vision-and-values/ or scan the code.

*Children's Health Queensland–Values Launch*

## National Disability Insurance Scheme

It strikes me that our approach to the NDIS came from a transitional mindset. We had gone from 'normal' life to one involving a significant disability at the very point in time when the new national disability scheme was taking shape.

Anyone who has lived with a disability since birth will probably be all too familiar with the old state and territory models of support. Again and again, in conversations with NDIS-eligible clients, I've been told stories about 'the old days', when the state authority would magnanimously bestow allowances upon the client, who was expected to be ever-grateful, no matter how limited the allowances were. The new scheme started rolling out across the country in 2016, but in my experience, many people remain unaware that as an NDIS client they can, and actually should, assume control of determining what support they need, and how they get it. The client has the power to advocate for and demand what they need (not want) to be able to have equitable access to life. There is still plenty of work to be done in educating people about how the NDIS should work for them.

For our part, we had no idea to begin with what the NDIS would or wouldn't fund. In 2016/17, when we were making plans for Samuel's discharge, the rollout hadn't yet reached our area. Campaign for Samuel Inc. was established to ensure support for him, regardless of what the NDIS would do. If the NDIS didn't cover his needs, then C4S Inc. would need to pick up the shortfall as we 'Built a Better Future for Samuel'.

Early on, we tried to make sense of the six so-called 'functional domains' (mobility, communication, social interaction, self-management, learning and self-care) that are at the heart of the NDIS assessment and planning processes. We quickly realised that the best way forward was not to use the scheme's generic planning documents but to dig deeper into the nitty-gritty of each of the different domains and pitch our arguments for Samuel's support needs against these. We brainstormed every single thing that might conceivably be needed in order to give NDIS planners as big a picture of our situation as we could. On the front cover of our submission, we included Samuel's name in a large font and two photos of Samuel and Amelia together—one from before his illness and one after. We wanted to give the NDIS planner a visible connection to Samuel both during and after our meeting with them.

Under advice, we insisted on a face-to-face planning meeting, rather than an over-the-phone, 'not-realising-I've-just-had-my-planning-meeting' meeting. In preparing our first planning submission, we also:

- Attended an NDIS information session, which offered useful tips and strategies.
- Added to our website's 'cascade' fundraising diagram whatever we could conceivably imagine that Samuel would need for his daily life, and what he would need to thrive.
- Tried to figure out what the NDIS 'functional domains' are and what each one covers. According to the scheme's own website, these six functional domains 'aim to capture how a disability impacts upon all aspects of a patient's life... and provide a practical and holistic framework within which to contextualise a person's disability and to understand the type and level of support an individual requires to live well.' Sounds simple, but this part was hideous.

- Mapped our list of what we needed against the domains, with reasons why each list item was needed.
- Learned to frame everything we were asking for in terms of 'reasonable and necessary' in providing 'choice and control'—key criteria considered by NDIS planners in the decision-making process.
- Packaged our 'wish list' (arranged by domains) into a document that included a potted summary of Samuel's story. This narrative included details of the activities he had enjoyed and participated in prior to his illness, and explicit details about his post-TM disability and the implications for his daily life into the future.

Our first meeting was long, but our efforts bore fruit—and sooner than we expected.

We chose to self-manage Samuel's NDIS plan to give us as much flexibility as possible, but it does add to our workload. We track our spending on a spreadsheet (mapped against the domains—we've nearly figured them all out) in case we are ever audited. It also gives us a good idea of where the supports need to come in future plans. We are currently working through issues agreed in October 2019 at COAG (Coalition of Australian Governments). There are some supports that cross over into the domain of health (NDIS is for disability *not* health) for participants who are defined as 'chronic but stable'. These include people like Samuel, who have complex medical needs such as 24-hour ventilation, or even just nightly ventilation support, and who require around-the-clock care.

## NDIS–Summary

For what it's worth, I would also offer the following tips for anyone trying to navigate the NDIS:
- Find out what support options may be available to you (through NDIS or other providers).
- Understand that the NDIS puts you in control of your life direction.

- Become comfortable with and get to know the scheme's language. The phrases 'choice and control' and 'reasonable and necessary' should be deployed at any suitable opportunity, especially during planning.

- At least try to get a feel for the different NDIS domains—it will help you formulate your initial application and subsequent planning submissions.

- The NDIS will allow for a more competitive market—exploit this. Clients in the past were limited in their choice of support agencies and sometimes suffered substandard care as a result. The 'choice and control' idea that is at the heart of the NDIS means care providers need to improve the quality of their services in order to keep their clients from going elsewhere.

- The self-managed option offers maximum choice and control, but it isn't for everyone.

- Be prepared to advocate for yourself.

- You have a voice. How you choose to use it is up to you, but as the saying goes, you catch more flies with honey than you do with vinegar.

- Don't presume your NDIS planner understands your particular situation and needs. Be explicit in unpacking what each day looks like for you.

- Don't make the mistake of underplaying your need for help during your planning meetings. Showing vulnerability, while focussing on your goals, is important.

- For subsequent annual planning meetings, don't presume the NDIS planner will be familiar with all of your background information. Be prepared to paint the picture at each plan review as clearly as possible, focussing not on the disability so much as what the day-to-day implications and needs are as a result of that disability. The NDIS planner needs to understand the *impact* of the disability and potential *outcomes* of the planned support.

# Samuel

## Our Resolve

I've already described how, in the early days, the hospital rehab staff focussed on working with the things Samuel *could* still do. His right big toe showed promise. And, as it became apparent that he hadn't been affected cognitively, it was heartening to know he would still have his intelligence, humour and his genuine concern for others. We wanted to make the best of whatever was available.

A social worker remarked one day, that because of our commitment, Samuel wouldn't just survive, he would thrive. These words played on my mind for a long time. I guess that's exactly what was unfolding. Surviving was baseline. Thriving was the real endgame, but it required a strong baseline. Samuel's future relies on a complex survival regime that must be firmly in place before the good stuff can happen.

## Surviving

The basics are simple but vital. Samuel relies on a ventilator 24/7 and without it, he will die. He relies on enteral feeding, so if this isn't done, he will starve to death. But how do we know that all his needs are met, without any negative impacts on his health? The answer is that Samuel's dietary and ventilation requirements must be regularly assessed by his treating teams.

Diet should be the easiest part: Weigh Samuel in his chair, weigh the chair and find the difference. Sounds straightforward, but think for a second: Who has a set of scales that can cater for the 250-plus kilograms of a teenage boy and his powerchair? And if we found them, what are the chances they would be conveniently located near a hoist to lift Samuel while the chair is weighed without him? In the end, it was simpler to buy an 'inline' set of scales that connect into his hoist apparatus. Trouble is, when the scales are connected, we can't raise Samuel high enough to get him fully off the bed. Instead, we need to hoist him, then lower him to the floor, connect the scales, weigh him, then lower him back to the floor, disconnect the scales, then lift him back into the bed. Only then do we have the information the dieticians require to track Samuel's BMI and provide advice and guidance on his nutritional needs.

As soon as we could, we switched from the continuous feed process used early on in PICU and established 'bolus' feeds delivered at regular mealtimes. The result, as expected, was digestive regularity. We believed this was better for his health, as well as being more convenient to work in with other regular routines.

An overnight sleep study is required at least once a year to ensure Samuel's ventilation settings are optimum. With cables connected to his head and body, Samuel labours through his annual 'lack-of-sleep study', as we call them, so that his ventilator pressures, breath rates and air volumes can all be assessed and adjusted depending on the oxygen and carbon dioxide levels in his system.

Surviving also entails other routine 'maintenance'. The less 'load-bearing' a person is, the more calcium leeches from their bones. This is not only bad for bone density, raising the risk of fractures, but it can lead to renal problems and the formation of kidney stones. Samuel uses two forms of therapy at home (alternating weekly) to address this. One is a tilt table. The other is a functional electrical stimulation (FES) cycling machine. Once he's safely strapped in, the tilt table, as the name suggests, raises Samuel to an almost upright position. With the FES, he lies on his bed, feet attached to the pedals, while electrodes carefully positioned on his leg muscles—glutes, quads, calves, hamstrings—help him to pedal. This regular exercise routine increases blood flow, strengthens his working muscles and keeps his bones strong.

Although each therapy session may only last twenty minutes or so, the process of setting up, getting Samuel into position, and then packing up afterwards, takes about an hour. It also takes two people, and Samuel's ventilator and connections must be carefully monitored. As the tilt table goes up, so does his tracheostomy, and so the ventilator circuits must follow.

Occasionally, something will go wrong with Samuel's body, or he will get sick. Prevention is definitely better than cure, and we try, if at all possible, to avoid more time in hospital. Sadly, a chest infection will put Samuel back in intensive care for at least two weeks; to recruit his lungs and fight infections requires the intricate, decidedly non-portable, intensive care ventilators. So, keeping him healthy is critical.

This also includes looking after his mental health. Navigating the tricky teenage years can be difficult for any young person, let alone someone with a complex disability like Samuel's. And it's an uncomfortable truth that the spectre of suicide hovers quietly at the back of all of our minds. It is a highly divisive issue, but one that disproportionately affects people with serious disabilities—so it is something that needs to be more widely discussed. While it is incredibly difficult, we have as a family become more comfortable in discussing our mental health, and we continue to pursue timely and appropriate support for Samuel and ourselves.

From the time Samuel came home, he has had a basic level of assistance provided by support workers. These staff, under arrangements determined at the time of discharge, were primarily responsible for ensuring his ventilation and dietary needs were met—the critical stuff. This was enough to meet the requirements for discharge, but in a sense it only moved the location of his 'surviving' from an institution to a family home. Don't get me wrong, we would far rather have Samuel at home than in hospital, but we wanted more—we wanted him to thrive.

## Thriving

Thankfully, Samuel's support workers have been trained in more than just ventilation and feeding. They carry out the maintenance and cleaning of suction units and other equipment; they know how to prepare for an outing during their shift; and they can carry out the complex process of hoisting and transferring him from chair to bed etc. Get all of these routine needs met and 'survival' is assured. Thriving, on the other hand, continues to be about dissolving barriers, facilitating solutions and meticulous planning to ensure Samuel can access the opportunities he chooses without the restrictions caused by his disability. As we promised, it is about doing whatever it takes.

Samuel's biggest success so far has been surviving the malady which befell him. Aside from making sure he went to school and did his homework, neither Jane nor I can claim credit for his academic successes, including being named Dux of his Junior School in grade nine. Likewise, when he took up boccia, we bought the necessary equipment and drove him to training, but it was he who developed the strategies and skills that would make him Queensland champion in his classification.

The challenges continue to lie in access. Will the university where he is keen to pursue a degree in business and/or legal studies be designed well enough for him to navigate and manoeuvre? How easy will it be to make long-haul flights—a necessity if he wants to represent Australia at international boccia competitions? The flight to Canberra in Year 6 was short enough that toileting could be managed pre- and post-flight. Transferring him from seat to commode mid-flight is likely impossible, and any alternative will involve overcoming a huge mental hurdle, given that he is actually continent.

Spontaneity will continue to be difficult. There will always be a minimum amount of preparation required for any change of routine—even a trip to the shops. And it's not just about equipment—Samuel's support workers have become pretty good at getting things ready in a hurry. But currently a big barrier to spontaneity is the shift schedule: In most cases, Samuel needs to be at home for support-worker changeovers. In other instances, newer support workers might not yet have the skills or confidence to leave the house with Samuel. And so there are only small windows of time in which spontaneous brainwaves can be indulged. 'Planned spontaneity', oxymoron though it may be, is the best we can do for now.

The rest of Samuel's future is purely speculative. And ours too. But we will continue to strategise and problem-solve—and cross just one bridge at a time. Most importantly, we want both of our children to be happy.

# Strangers

## The Very Fabric

The goal for Samuel is that he will one day live independently of us and be able to advocate to his support workers for what he needs and wants. Of course, he is well aware his life-threatening vulnerability means he will at least need to tolerate the presence of others in his home; hopefully, these relationships will be positive ones. The role that any potential 'significant other' may play in this mix is a complete unknown; certainly, the dynamic would be very different with a life partner sharing his journey. As Samuel enters his mid-teens, we are on a trajectory where his independence is slowly increasing while our parental guidance role, as for all young adults, gradually diminishes.

We live with other people in our home, day and night. The burden of care is so great that not to have them would be ridiculous, but to stay empowered about our need to have them in our home takes some hefty navigation. 'I don't know how you cope having other people in your house all of the time,' is a remark I've heard so often, I thought it worth finishing our story with some thoughts on this.

From the old adage, we know that love is the key ingredient that makes a house a home. But it's more than that. If 'I' am always the central person in any relationship that I have, then clearly, in the family home, each of us is central and we each have a connecting relationship with the other people in the house. I believe these relationships are defined simply by what we do and what we say. How we act with and around each other is as important as the different conversations we have.

These interpersonal interactions form a tapestry—the very fabric of the family. But within the home, this fabric can be stretched and pulled in ways it never would be in public. Home is the sanctuary where actions and conversations can be challenged safely. It is the place where moral and ethical positions can be debated without necessarily being embraced as a firm belief or rejected.

There are elements that add to, or even challenge, the strength and stability of the sanctuary that is our family home. These include predictability of routines, boundaries, expectations and discipline, respectful turn-taking, manners and courtesy, quiet times, private times, day-to-day stresses, forgiveness, humour, laughter, and love.

The inescapable fact is that the strangers in our home see and hear *all* of this—the good stuff, and the bad. Real life is messy.

How they engage with this—or more accurately, don't engage—is what determines whether this fabric remains essentially ours, and private. By far the hardest skill for a support worker to master is knowing how to act 'in the third person'. While they get to go home after their shift, leaving the complexity of our family life behind them, they are human, too. Their personalities will influence how difficult it is for them to melt into the background when necessary, but it remains true that the less intrusive they are, the less stress we feel.

This concept of this fabric applies elsewhere, too—at school, going shopping or even at the off-leash dog park. While different environments each have their own unique fabric, let me explain how it works in our home.

## A Fundamental Approach

As readers will have gathered, I found it difficult to cope with having other people in our home. There were many reasons for this, and I wrestled with my pain and anger. To be clear, I did not, and have not, *ever* resented the support workers. Mostly, they do their work diligently, with care for Samuel while being mindful of the impact their presence has in our home. However, while I am more accepting now, I have, at times, resented the *reasons* that have determined *why* we need them.

The change for us all has been enormous. Samuel's debilitation was sudden, unexpected, severe—and had profound implications. Coming to terms with the realisation that he would not 'recover', and that his life expectancy might be impacted, was sobering.

In the earlier days, my stress levels would bubble over when support workers seemed unable to 'read the room'—to actively understand what was happening at any given point—and when they interrupted in such a way as to show disrespect to the fabric of our family life. Worse, was if they interrupted to ask a question about something that was clearly spelled out in the information documents that Jane had spent hundreds of hours preparing and keeping up to date. Hardest of all was if I felt Jane, or the work she had done, was being disrespected.

Other provocations included Samuel's needs being placed second to whatever other job was being done at the time; or if alarms weren't silenced as soon as possible; or when support workers couldn't seem to help hoist Samuel the same way from one day to the next. At times, it all seemed so difficult that not having support workers even looked like the better option.

Something quite small, on top of many other small issues building up, could trigger me. Jane knew the signs. Me suddenly leaving a support worker to continue shower preparations with Samuel by themselves would signal to her that I was near breaking point. If I put on my runners and headed for the door, an eruption was imminent. I tried to put some distance between the house and myself before the emotions gushed forth, hoping that the gathering dusk and the sound of my footsteps would mask the worst of the breakdown. At times, it just wasn't working for me.

But we had to have these people in our home. Going it alone was not an option. I needed to accept them into our home environment. We all needed it to work. But how?

As a starting point, we needed to consider two fundamental questions—ones that are specifically relevant to us: In everyday family life, what would we, as parents, be doing for Samuel, or he for himself, if he hadn't been paralysed? And, because he *is* paralysed, how much more than that is it fair and reasonable for us to do?

These were painful questions to even contemplate—how could we even begin to reconcile parental responsibility with these new circumstances? And for Samuel, why should he feel like a burden when the paralysis was not even remotely his fault? As parents it was natural for us to choose to do *more* for him than we would if he was able-bodied, but a support worker stepping in and offering first, without being asked, really was what we needed.

Offers of assistance, particularly when working with children, are best when they are specific and not open-ended. 'Would you like me to do something?' is not as helpful as, 'Would you like me to write down your questions?' or, 'Would you like me to clean your glasses then set up the iPad?' A young person in Samuel's position, learning how to advocate for themselves, in ways they should never have been expected to do, will benefit from specific modelling of examples of what they might ask for. A child may feel awkward asking their adult carers for help, so showing them the sorts of things they can ask, and ways to break down requests into smaller parts, can lessen any feeling of embarrassment or of being a burden. They can see that small requests are very reasonable and achievable.

The age and maturity of the child are complicating factors that support workers need to consider. The preferences and ground rules set down by parents also need to be taken into account when considering a young client's requests for assistance. For example, if the parents have a rule about no screen devices after 8:30pm, the question becomes who is at fault if this rule is broken? Is it the child for asking the support worker to set up the tablet or computer for them? Or is it the support worker for going along with the request?

A thoughtful response encourages a gradual release of responsibility from the support worker to the child—allowing them not only to take on responsibility for themselves as they grow and mature, but to develop a healthy acceptance of the situation in which they find themselves.

Our concept of how it would, or should, look to have support workers in our home, was driven by the fundamental questions posed above. These people would be doing the things that Samuel would have done for himself, but couldn't.

Inevitably, there were gaps.

CHQ at Home training primarily focussed on Samuel's ventilation needs. This included his ventilator, tracheostomy, airways suctioning, and other tasks clearly linked to these things. We didn't ever see a prescribed list of tasks on any job description, but we were given to understand that jobs like showering Samuel, for example, could be done by a ventilation support worker when Samuel was ready for this. By the time he was ready to have non-family members perform such an intimate task, CHQ support workers were clearly of the view that it was not within the scope of their duties. Gradually, the role description changed more and more to being almost exclusively around trache/vent tasks.

The growing gap between what we needed and what was being offered caused significant stress. Over time, this has gradually been resolved with the transition to NDIS-funded support workers whose job descriptions encompass a broader range of tasks. Nevertheless, we continued to be extremely grateful for the CHQ at Home service, knowing that without it, Samuel might still be in hospital.

## Within the Context of the Family

Regardless of who the service provider might be, we all recognise that the support workers have a job to do. Adulthood is fast approaching, and the goal is for Samuel to eventually manage and direct his support team by himself. The support he has received since discharge has been in the context of this journey, and it has been tailored to meet his changing needs.

Ultimately, it is always about how Samuel has his needs met in a timely way. In the interim, it is about how *we* as parents want his needs to be met in order to assist him on his road to autonomy. And in the beginning, it was also about what we, as parents, needed.

Jane seemed instinctively to be able to judge the skill level of individual support workers and figure out how to work with them to bring out their best. She quickly grasped that although new workers came to us equipped with a certain level of skill and knowledge, they required further on-the-job nurturing and development in order to excel.

I, on the other hand, expected their training regime to have furnished them with *absolutely everything* they needed to know to do their job faultlessly. So it was frustrating that Jane needed to spend so much time supporting them. Surely, they should know! Their training had obviously not been up to scratch!

This was both naïve and unreasonable.

After their initial training and orientation, new support workers normally complete a number of 'buddy shifts' with an experienced worker who is familiar with Samuel's needs and routines.

This makes for a good start. But to do their job really well, they need to get to know the nature of our family. And this takes time. It is not something most people can do straight away. It's embarrassing to admit, but it was only after I started writing about the role of support workers for this book that I finally understood and accepted this.

My expectations were so unattainably high, they were simply unfair. For me, there was no middle ground in which support workers could learn and develop their skills—it was either pass or fail. At times, all I could muster in terms of constructive feedback was an unhealthy dose of passive-aggressive language and action—the sort of petulant, childish behaviour I would have found unacceptable in my professional life.

As I thought more about it, I realised that good carers seemed to progress through four discrete levels on their path to becoming great at what they need to do: Training, Compliance, Understanding, and Invisibility. Once I'd identified these levels, it became clear that there would be markers or indicators that would enable staff (and me) to see *how* to move from one to the next. Understanding where they were in their learning allowed me to be more patient and to know how to help them move to the next level.

Here's a brief primer on each of the levels.

## Training

At this level, new workers complete the basic training provided by their employer. To work with a child such as Samuel, this training covers all things within the scope of paediatric mechanical ventilation and tracheostomy management. They need to demonstrate a competency to their employer, showing they are able to successfully look after a client's life-support needs. They will have been identified by their employer as a potential 'match' for the client—based on what is known about the family.

## Compliance

At this level, staff apply their training to monitor and maintain a safe level of care for their client. They complete routine tasks and follow instructions as outlined by the client (and the client's parents) as well as those mandated by their employer.

## Understanding

To be successful at this level, support workers will firstly need to be comfortable with the technical and routine aspects of their job. As they settle into their role, they will hopefully also develop an understanding of the reasons behind most, if not all, of the routines and tasks they carry out. In a family like ours, such routines may have evolved from a combination of basic family expectations and experience, as well as many months of trial and error. Some may be grounded in practical reasons, while others may reflect a family preference. At this level, individual support workers may be entrusted to make adjustments to routines, processes or practices, as long as they remain true to the intent and reasoning behind them—and as long as they are not detrimental to the expectations of the family or other support workers. What this level looks like in practice may vary a great deal between families.

## Invisibility

At this level, support workers with a thorough grasp of their role and an understanding of the expectations required, may be entrusted to make autonomous adjustments to routines and practices based on their knowledge of the reasoning behind them. Through observation, truly great workers are able to recognise the interactions between family members that make up the private fabric of family life. They are thoughtful, and self-aware enough to be able to 'read the room' and to know when to step out of a situation, whether it's a disagreement between family members, a discussion about what to do on a Sunday afternoon, or a regular family meal. This level is aspirational but achievable.

A thoughtful support worker might also ask themselves: 'Is there a way I can do this task, or a way that I can behave, that will be less intrusive?' They will hopefully also be mindful of how actions they take in the course of a shift can impact on other members of the support team.

I make no apologies for having high expectations, but my timeframes needed adjusting. Naturally, new carers need time to settle into their role and to learn our family ways before they can have any hope of achieving a level of 'invisibility'.

For the team members who joined us when Samuel first came home, the task was made even more difficult by the fact that our family was 'resetting' itself. Having a framework like the one I've described would have made it easier for me to be more patient and understanding.

Perhaps my analysis won't be helpful for everyone, but if nothing else, I hope it may enable others to avoid the mistakes I made, and to improve understanding on both sides of the support worker-client relationship.

The process of writing has helped me to purge much of the negativity burning inside me: my resentment that we *needed* these 'strangers' in our home; and my unreasonable expectations about their ability to carry out their roles.

I have also started a list of all of the 'positives' that are the result of Samuel's support workers being part of our lives. As time goes on, I will have more to add, but I began with these:

- They provide overnight monitoring, so that everyone in the family can get a good night's sleep.
- They carry out hoisting and transfers between bed and chairs (wheelchair and shower chair).
- They dress Samuel and carry out routine personal hygiene tasks—teeth cleaning, face washing, hair brushing—as well as toileting and showering.
- They make positional adjustments for Samuel in his chair and bed so that he is always comfortable.
- They perform range-of-motion exercises to keep his limbs supple.
- They set up the assistive technologies that Samuel uses for increased independence and leisure—iPad, Xbox.
- They respond to the different alarms emitted by Samuel's equipment (providing auditory relief for Jane and me—we still hear them, but we don't need to worry as much).
- They engage in all sorts of dynamic and stimulating conversations with Samuel.
- They foster Samuel's self-advocacy skills, allowing him to grow in confidence with them.

Everyone knows that while it is great to have visitors—whether family or friends—it's also great to see them leave. And if you've ever had visitors who stayed a few days too long, you've probably had a small taste of what it's like to have workers around you all the time.

What are the things you do in your own home that you wouldn't do if someone else was there?

Even after all the modifications and improvements, our house is not so different from most people's—and the walls are very thin. Add a support worker into the mix, and imagine all the things that might suddenly become awkward: personal conversations (especially if they're about someone in the house); loud and unrepentant flatulence (exposing some serious dietary issues); some marital intimacy... I'm sure you get the idea.

The ritual of waking up and walking outside to get the weekend papers in nothing more than boxer shorts becomes awkward enough, without the added embarrassment of being caught absent-mindedly scratching one's bits. The tradition of waking a family member on their birthday by jumping on their bed first thing, all of us in our daggiest pyjamas, is now also just a memory.

Having other people in our home all the time is complex and challenging for all of us, but it is Samuel who has had to make the biggest adjustment. He has an adult with him at home, at school, day in, day out—even while he is sleeping. For the moment, until he is old enough to dismiss our services, we will try to give him what respite from strangers we can. We will try to teach him how to manage his helpers. And we will try to balance our need for a private family life with the respite Samuel's support workers provide—which enables us to just keep going.

## Strangers–Summary

- The home and family are made up of the interactions between the people in them: the conversations, the actions, the silences, the inaction.
- For families like ours, having other people physically around us is an inescapable reality. Perhaps one day, robots will fill some support roles, but in the meantime, families that cannot reconcile themselves to having strangers in their home, will have to go it alone.

- Families may still be determining their fundamental approach to support and working out what they believe they are entitled to or what they should have. Tread carefully—during this transitional period, families may be experiencing a roller-coaster ride of emotions like grief or anger. This may well make it difficult for them to express their appreciation for the service their support workers provide.

- Good support workers strive to work seamlessly together and support the family's needs through:
    - Becoming competent at operating any equipment and applying medical/health supports
    - Following instructions and processes, understanding that this is key to making everything 'work'. They focus their attention on the client's needs
    - Understanding the reasons behind the processes, routines and systems, and using this knowledge to exercise some discretion in the fulfillment of their role. This needs to be done without compromising the systems themselves or the capacity of other support workers (including parents) to undertake tasks in consistent ways. An example of this would be returning items to the place they belong after use so that workers on later shifts can find them
    - Being aware enough of family interactions to avoid accidentally or deliberating inserting themselves into situations that don't involve them. Being aware of how their own behaviour can impact on family life.

- The best support workers typically ask themselves: 'Is there a way I can do this, or behave, that will be less intrusive to the family's life?' and, 'Is there a way I can do this, or behave, that will be mindful or supportive of the needs of the other support workers in the team?'

- If your client is a young child, it is helpful to be specific when phrasing offers of assistance. Through good modelling, you can show them ways to self-advocate more articulately, and reassure them that their requests are not impositions. The situation may well change as the child matures. If the family's goal is for the young person to be more independent in asking for what they need—to take ownership of their own situation—then a less proactive approach may be required.

- New clients and families may not have the language to describe their needs or to channel their emotions. They may need support in understanding how to do this. Although patience in such situations is appreciated, clients need to remember that the support worker is not to blame for their predicament—displays of anger or frustration are never appropriate.

- With the arrival of the NDIS, the provision of services will continue to become more competitive. As NDIS participants increasingly exercise their right to choose, it will undoubtedly exert pressure on providers to improve the quality of the services they offer.

- It sucks—but it is a necessary suck—to have 'strangers' in our home, and so we try to remember the positives. We are reminded of these 'positives' whenever a support nightshift gets cancelled—that really sucks! Another positive is the 'added value' that many support workers bring to the family. For us, the deep conversations Samuel has with so many support workers, especially at night, brings us joy. He values their conversational contributions and they, his.

- In the end, this is all about building a better future for Samuel. We will do whatever it takes—and we are never ever going to give up.

# Epilogue

After her repatriation to Maryborough Hospital in 2016, Mum required ongoing support. My brothers were able to find her a place in a retirement home in Hervey Bay. Despite continuing therapy for her ankle, she never fully regained her mobility, and she suffered a number of small strokes. In mid-2019 she had a significant stroke, and in December of that year she passed away. Our family did manage a trip to see her in January 2018—the first time she saw Samuel after his hospitalisation was also the last. It was confronting for Mum to see Samuel in his wheelchair with the ventilator and all manner of paraphernalia, but she took it in her stride and with a great deal of admiration for Samuel's strength of character. She was so proud of both Amelia and Samuel.

In 2020, we were sad to learn of the passing of Dexter, the beautiful West Highlander therapy dog who'd been a regular visitor to Samuel's bedside in PICU. Dexter, with his owner Tanya's wonderful support, brought us priceless moments of peace and normality throughout Samuel's treatment.

After the Canberra trip, we followed up with the Australian War Memorial about the accessibility issues we experienced. The management explained that while their elevators meet Australian standards for wheelchair accessibility, the dimensions of the elevator to the Shrine of Remembrance are limited by the building's heritage listing. Nevertheless, they have embraced the challenge of coming up with a solution for future visits—either by Samuel or others with similar needs—and have offered to hire a 'stair climber' whenever needed to solve the problem. They also sent a wonderful hamper for the 2017 Trivia Night raffle.

We continue to navigate the transition from CHQ at Home support to NDIS-funded support. This is exceedingly complex and time-consuming. We will continue to work with the children's hospital for medical interventions and supports for the time being, but will need to transition to the support provided by the Princess Alexandra Hospital spinal unit around the time Samuel turns 18.

Campaign for Samuel Incorporated continues in its quest to be 'Building a Better Future' for Samuel. As it has become clearer what role the NDIS will play in his life, there is no question that the Campaign will still be required. Although we will continue to do our best to ensure Samuel's needs are well-presented to the NDIS, funding will still only cover that which is 'reasonable and necessary' to provide 'choice and control' for participants. Campaign for Samuel will continue to augment this funding as an additional measure of quality and support for Samuel and the family. We continue to be grateful for the hundreds of wonderful people who have contributed to the campaign; many of them are known to us, but many others are not. Whether they've donated money, goods or services, or just their time and love, it is all valued.

* If you'd like to donate, you can visit www.campaignforsamuel.org.au. Donations of $2 or more to The Samuel Thorne Fund in a financial year are tax deductible for Australian taxpayers.

Out of her 2019 graduating cohort at Griffith University, Amelia was the first to be offered a job as a midwife within a service model called

Midwifery Group Practice. She believes strongly in continuity of care for her mothers-to-be, and for them to have informed control over their treatment and support. My unbiased opinion is that she is an exceptional midwife.

Samuel had spinal-rodding surgery in August 2019 to correct his worsening scoliosis. He was under general anaesthetic for more than five hours. The procedure involved metal rods being inserted in his back to straighten out the twists and sags in his spine. Following the surgery, he'd grown about ten centimetres. Besides making him look more like the young man he was becoming, the extra height made it necessary to tilt his chair a great deal when getting in and out of the car. A purchase order for a new modified vehicle that could safely accommodate his changing needs swiftly followed.

In 2019, the National Boccia Titles were held in Brisbane. Samuel, as first-time captain, led his Queensland Boccia Pair to a national bronze medal in the BC3 division. He was also named 2019 Queensland champion in this division. Covid-19 upended plans for the national 2020 competition, which was to have been held in Hobart, but in late 2020 Samuel successfully defended his Queensland title. Samuel was also named as the 2019 Sporting Wheelies and Disabled Association Junior Male Athlete of the Year.

The routine hygiene practices that are now part of our daily life meant we were in a surprisingly good position when the Covid-19 pandemic took hold in Australia. We were obviously fearful about what dangers the virus could hold for Samuel, but we also dreaded what might happen if either a family member or a support worker tested positive. This would have meant an enforced halt to our support worker services, leaving us to cope on our own, 24-7, for at least two weeks until any quarantine measures were completed.

Jane continues to amaze and inspire me and many others. Keeping on top of all that needs doing for Samuel is a fulltime job: it involves ensuring medical equipment is maintained; supplies are ordered; Samuel's school drop-off and pick-up; tracking and processing our NDIS purchases; and much more. Somehow, she manages to juggle everything that Samuel's daily life entails, while still finding time to maintain a deeply loving, supportive relationship with Amelia far away in central Queensland. I could never have asked for a better mother for our children, and I know I won the lottery when she accepted my proposal of marriage all those years ago. I am so grateful for her love—and also her patience.

I have taught myself some basics of CAD drawing with the aim of being able to design and 3D-print parts and objects to improve Samuel's quality of life. I've experimented with better ways to mount switches and other devices on Samuel's wheelchair, as well as looking for ways that his Xbox controller can be better mounted on his footplate for when he's gaming. Problem-solving like this helps me feel that I am still able to make worthwhile contributions to Samuel's day-to-day life. And I really love the times when he and I just connect: a smile, a nod, a quick chat. Our father-son connection looks nothing like I once expected it would—I like to think it's better. It is grounded in collective experiences that none of us would wish upon anyone else, but that all of us have worked through together. And my inspiration has always been Samuel himself. In 2018, I took up a deputy principal position in the Queensland Children's Hospital School with my prime role being to support the education staff working in hospital programs throughout the state. These stretch from the Gold Coast to Cairns and west to Toowoomba and support a diverse range of students—some in paediatric wards as well as adolescents in mental health inpatient units and day programs.

Soon after Samuel's discharge, on some of our happier days, we plundered the family's Memory Jar. We revelled in the positivity it brought. After reading them, we disposed of most of the notes as a way of moving forward, keeping just a few for the jar. We didn't need to hold onto these artifacts of positive memories to reaffirm just how great our family was. We are strong in the love and knowledge of our bonds.

Often, each day is still just a really hard slog. I continue to take time to honour my grief, although I find I don't need to do this as much these days. If I need to let a few emotions flow, just so they don't build up too much, I find it helpful to read back over sections of this book. Reliving the experience in this way doesn't feel like a negative, but rather something that helps me deal better with my emotions and with life.

And in any case, at any time, I can hover in space. I can float above the eucalypts on a misty morning with my family. I can liberate my heart and mind whenever I choose by visiting 'My Special Place'.

# Part 4–The Text Message Updates

Updates about Samuel's progress sent out to family and friends since 30 November 2015 on admission to Lady Cilento Children's Hospital until discharge.

**2015**

### 30.11.15   Day 1

Hi guys some worrying news to share. Samuel is very unwell and been admitted to Lady Cilento hospital where he will remain for a number of weeks... a month... months maybe. Diagnosis is Transverse Myelitis which has affected his ability to use his arms, control his neck, breathe on his own and more... His immune system is attacking the nerve cells. Has been put into an induced coma.  Talk soon, thoughts and prayers appreciated. Love Thornes

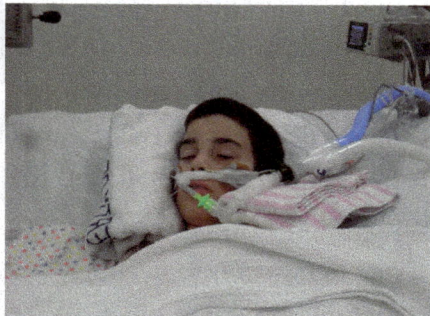

### 03.12.15   Day 4

Samuel's update, eyes open and looked at TV screen for 10mins this morning. Physio continues twice a day and antibiotics taken to address pneumonia. No improvement in health since Monday, so under general anaesthetic in the pm to insert vascular catheter in preparation for blood washing procedures over the next week starting tomorrow to replace antibodies. While under, also

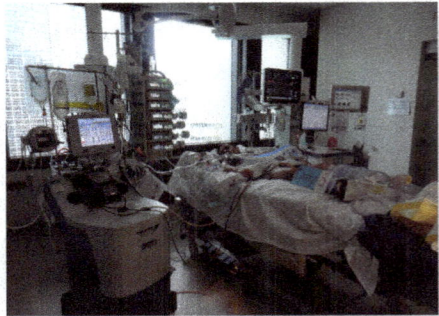

replacing oral respirator tube with nasal tube. Have yes/no answering system operating with eye blinking which is working well when lucid. Day 5 awaits. BTW no reply needed

**04.12.15   Day 5**

Moved to room 26, much quieter and has windows for natural light. Samuel's first plasmapheresis treatment lasted about 4 hours. Listened to music through the procedure. He coped quite well, blinking to let staff know when uncomfortable

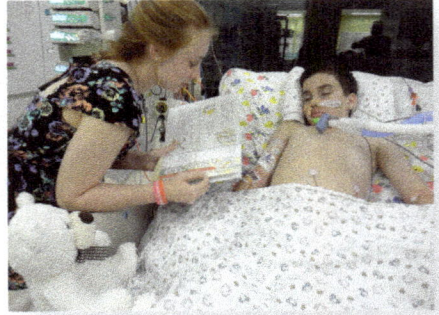

from a side effect of treatment. Thank heavens for blinking. Sponge bath to freshen him up. Late this afternoon he moved his foot at little side to side. Great! Acknowledged to Amelia he had been practising/ trying to more his foot... hopefully still happening tomorrow:) Resting peacefully...very tired...huge day.

**06.12.15   Day 7**

Samuel has been resting a lot today. Been in pain in arms and legs, meds being increased slightly to stop him feeling uncomfortable. Physio twice today has given him a good work out. Left toes a little bit of movement which is positive. Plasmapheresis again tomorrow. One long week down. XO

**07.12.15   Day 8**

Samuel had a restful day. Physio twice and second round of plasmapheresis which went like clock-work today. Visited by occupational therapist who made temporary splints for both hands. Take care XO

**08.12.15   Day 9**

Samuel has more movement in left toes and in right leg. Physio gave him 1 good work out and one gentle workout. Tried without an extra dose of pain killer on the first session, however he didn't cope well, so pain killer to be administered every time. Chest x-ray indicates pneumonia developed again, so back on antibiotics. Temperature up due to pneumonia is causing him discomfort. 3rd session of plasmapheresis, done over about 3 hours, slower session for his comfort today. Speech therapist has made up some pages to help with communication. Take care, and no reply needed. XO

**09.12.15   Day 10**

Physio this morning then Samuel wanted to watch TV...a shark show... right up his alley. Nice to see. Has had occupational therapist working on limbs. Plasmapheresis went efficiently. Been under anaesthetic to have nasal breathing tube and cuff replaced as problem with current cuff suspected. Santa visited today and is happy for a late email with Samuel's wish list:) Speech therapist tightening communication board prompts—working well this evening. Neurologist detected a reflex in right ankle, that's positive! Take care XO

**10.12.15   Day 11**

Quieter morning today. Visits from (actors) Dr O'Dear, Dr Wobble, a Santa Stormtrooper and Darth Vader—fun to look at and entertaining. Physio twice, OT made and fitted hand/wrist splints. Speech therapist amending communication boards. Samuel enjoyed more shark week TV. Major achievement was being moved to a special chair which he sat in reasonably upright for an hour and a half. This is great for his chest, almost equivalent to a physio session. Very exhausting afternoon. Was presented his age champion swimming medal by his Principal and Deputy Principal! Should sleep well tonight. XO

**11.12.15   Day 12**

Samuel slept well last night as expected. Had a busy day again. Last plasmapheresis (for now), went well and Samuel will be assessed again on Monday to see if more is required, depends on any changes. Physio says chest improving, and put him in the chair again in afternoon. A smoother transition, but still not wanted by Samuel. OT fixed splints for better fit on wrists/hands. Music therapist popped in and will call again on Monday to play some music with Samuel. Take care XO

**12.12.15   Day 13**

Quiet Saturday. Physio gave Samuel a workout, helped move him to the chair where he sat for close to 3 hours. Doesn't seem to mind it once settled, but not keen to move initially. Catheter removed to see if any bladder control. Has 12 hrs of monitoring, if working great, if not then catheter set up again. No breathing response as yet, fully ventilated still, doctors expect it may be weeks before any change. Only time will tell. Take care. XO

**14.12.15   Day 15**

2 day update...Physio then Samuel sat in the chair for over 3 hours, watching TV and snoozing yesterday. Trying to decline medication for pain, but accepted a smaller dose. Catheter re-inserted as body not ready to use those muscles yet. ENT specialist spoke with us and then Samuel about a tracheostomy. This operation will occur later in the week... Probably Thursday...could be Wednesday. A tracheostomy is preferred to make the prolonged use of ventilators more comfortable and safe. Samuel is naturally unsure about this procedure, but we have assured him we will only do what's right for his health. Drs still deciding about more plasmapheresis. Waiting for neurologist to make final call. Another huge week ahead. XO

**15.12.15   Day 16**

Samuel enjoyed Music therapy today while sitting in chair. Met anaesthetist who will assist on tracheostomy operation tomorrow afternoon. Explanatory talk by ENT nurse who showed on doll what he will look like after tracheostomy. Samuel continues to be so brave, we're so proud if his patience/perseverence! Prayers for Samuel at 2pm tomorrow would be appreciated. Take care, XO

### 16.12.15   Day 17

Been a long day of waiting. Physio had him in the chair for couple of hours. Exhausted after this today. Expect he didn't have the best sleep, was awake 2 hours earlier than normal, was ready with a question to spell out about being able to breathe. Quite calm, settled and sleepy before surgery. In surgery from 3:15pm and back to us safely at 5:30pm. Thank you for your prayers and thoughts. ENT surgeons very happy with procedure. Thank you God for his safe return to us. Now on to a beautiful, smooth recovery, is our plan.

### 17.12.15   Day 18

Pain being managed well, tracheostomy looking good. Nervous about movement near his trachy, ... understandable. Samuel was able to move his head ever so slightly side to side, and up and down this morning...amazing! Challenging evening, Samuel felt he couldn't breathe, physio called in to help clear chest. A little medication about to be given and hopefully a calm restful night soon. We are all ready for bed tonight. XO

### 18.12.15   Day 19

Day 19 Samuel happy Craig got some av working in tv. Room change to 23. Physio had him pedalling legs on machine with his legs in slings. Machine doing all the work. Samuel used his big toe to tap drum in session with music therapist. Tracheostomy site sore and still getting used to it .... as expected.  Most amazing today....was seeing machine show that Samuel has triggered some breaths for about 2 hours. That's a great start. Hopefully he will do this again tomorrow, if only for a short time. Prayers are clearly being answered, thank you! XO :)

### 19.12.15   Day 20

Very quiet day today. Nothing new, no breaths being triggered today. Very tired, seems he didn't have a particularly good sleep last night. Hoping tonight he has a good sleep and is a little brighter tomorrow. Think today he was also ready for a weekend where he could just try to stop :) XO Some great Amelia news ... she received an OP of 3!!

**20.12.15   Day 21**

Been a quiet weekend, Samuel is well rested. Samuel hasn't really
wanted to engage with anyone, but hoping this will change when Physio,
OT, speech and music therapy all happen again tomorrow. Another room
change ... view of outside world ... maybe even fireworks at South Bank?
Room 03 still in PICU. Take care XO

**21.12.15   Day 22**

After a quiet weekend, Samuel has had a busy day. Started the day
in a happier mood thankfully. He read a few pages of his book which was
propped open in an acrylic recipe holder.  Watched a couple of minecraft
you tube recordings. Physio for his chest, then went on the special leg sling
cycling machine for about 20mins. Sat out in his chair for over 4 hours, 2 of
those hours out on the balcony in fresh air watching the outside world go by.
OT made a new splint  for right hand as a cannula was removed from that
wrist late last week. Music therapist played and sang for him this afternoon.
I wonder why he's tired? That's day 22 filled. XO

**22.12.15   Day 23**

A busy day...Physio on chest then .., cycling machine..3.5km covered
today! Samuel loved this and was looking forward to it.  a hospital dog
visited and sat on the end of Samuel's bed, where he patted the dog with
his foot. Wonderful! He sat out on balcony, enjoyed music therapy. Is
borrowing (hospital doesn't have one .... yet????) over Christmas, New Year
an 'Eye Gaze' calibrated to follow his eyes which will allow him to construct
sentences which can be converted to speech. Chose Her Majesty's QE2
voice. First sentence was 'Sam is awesome'. Quite enough for one day. XO

**23.12.15   Day 24**

What a roller coaster today has been. The great things definitely make
us move on from the lower points. Samuel had his first tracheostomy change
... daunting for all, but done. Samuel watched Christmas carols on Level 2 in
his new wheelchair, after being lifted by a hoist into the chair. 2 doctors and
2 nurses accompanied us, we felt Samuel was safe. Even better was Samuel
triggering breaths for much of the afternoon. So nice to see that again! XO

**24.12.15    Day 25**

Happy Christmas Eve! We hope you have a magical Christmas. We are planning a relaxing, fun, family day. Today Samuel received a special gift from his Physio ... an extra cycle session where he reached 7.22km in 30mins. What an early Christmas gift we received this morning when Samuel said 'hello Mum, happy Christmas Eve and hello Dad'. Tears of joy today that's for sure. As Samuel exhales the air escaping around his trachey tube enables him to try to speak a little:) Samuel's wheel chair was adjusted to fit his body better so should be more comfortable now. Thank you for your support/ love/prayers as we continue on this journey. Til Boxing Day.XO

**26.12.15    Day 27**

Well that was a Christmas and Boxing Day to experience only once. Samuel has done it tough with his ventilation these last 2 days, very anxious about not being able to breathe to his satisfaction on a different but not so noisy machine. This resulted in going back to the original ventilator and another tracheostomy tube replacement today. Basal lung collapse (minor), and antibiotics to help clear thick lung secretions. A very restful afternoon and we left him watching a movie ... very relaxed.

**27.12.15    Day 28**

After a pretty anxious last couple of days, Lungs looking improved again and minor collapse seems to be improving also. Catheter back in, body not ready for that function as yet. Tracheostomy / breathing issues saw trachy replaced on Saturday with a cuffed slightly bigger tube so no speech again for now. Hoping to pedal on cycling machine tomorrow. Quieter staff-wise due to many being on leave until early January. XO

**28.12.15    Day 29**

Samuel had a reasonably quiet day, spent 3.5 hours out in wheelchair, including on the balcony for about 2 hours. Left foot tiny movement to left and right...progress! Breathing not been triggered by Samuel for couple of days...but it will be again one day soon. One more quiet day then more staff back on deck to keep Samuel busy:) XO

### 29.12.15   Day 30

Day 30...an assorted day. Rehab team assessed progress to date— have a few plans re bladder, pain relief and are closely monitoring his range of movement. Physio and OT spent time moving his limbs/ joints. Need a good oiling:) Due to 3kg loss, have increased his feeds slightly and trialling giving it in bulk so more like a meal, 5 times a day. Reckon Samuel will need 6 times a day to take supper into account:) Highlight for today was Dexter the dog on Samuel's bed being foot patted for over an hour! Cycle day tomorrow...bring it on! Take care. XO

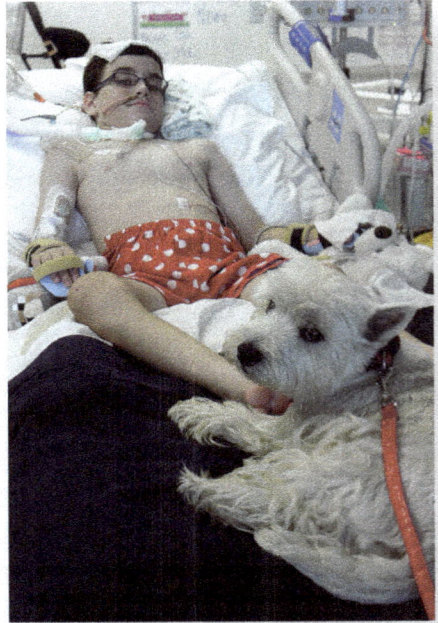

### 30.12.15   Day 31

Samuel keeps trying really hard with all that is asked of him. Cycling machine for 20mins today had him focussing on pedalling slowly concentrating on the muscles used to push and pull. He sat in the chair for over an hour which was quite exhausting. Hoping for a calmer night than last night. XO

### 2016

### 01.01.16   Day 32

Happy New Year! Samuel has had 2 good days. Yesterday was so busy doing everything the many specialists wanted Samuel to do. His reward was enjoying the fireworks from his room at 8:30pm and the nurse kindly woke him to see the midnight fireworks. Samuel has been smiling a lot these last 2 days. Trachy cuff has been deflated slightly for periods of time yesterday and today so he could speak to us. Will continue to share any significant updates as Samuel progresses, but will be reducing the frequency our general (daily) texts. Please continue to keep Samuel in your thoughts and prayers.  Thank you XO

### 04.01.16   Day 36

Dear family, Samuel has had 3 really happy days, taking everything in his stride. It was great to have all the specialist teams back today planning the goals for Samuel's week. Unfortunately he hit a bump in his progress at lunch time today, with a partial left lung collapse causing him distress knowing he couldn't get his breathing right. Here's hoping his road is a little smoother tomorrow. Love and prayers, XO

### 06.01.16   Day 38

Day 38 Samuel recovering well from Monday's partial lung collapse. Been busy since Monday with specialists. Tomorrow he will have an MRI and contrast dye MRI followed by lumbar puncture. We pray for a big difference in results between these procedures & ones on 29 Nov. No speech since Monday, hopefully in next day or so, he will be well enough for the trachy cuff to be partially/fully deflated again. Extensive testing today of sense of touch all over his body... soft, sharp/blunt—good results:) ; test of movement/muscles /and strength of these...very limited. His right foot scored well—sets a good example to the rest of his body. Special prayers for safe procedures tomorrow gratefully appreciated. Will message again when some results are known. XO.

### 07.01.16   Day 39

Samuel—MRI shows some improvement in spinal cord and brain stem. Good to know no antibodies in spinal fluid. Scarring of spinal cord not ruled out which could lead to some disability. Future MRI to confirm. Will be monitoring continuous improvements in movement and focussing on the positives. XO

### 11.01.16   Day 43

Samuel had a very settled weekend after a tough breathing patch early on Saturday. He enjoyed a trip in his chair to the balcony garden on

Sat. and Starlight entertainment room on Sun....despite not wanting to go. A very persuasive doctor initiated the excursions and accompanied us as reassurance. (along with another Dr & our nurse.) Week 7 had begun busily ...timetable is quite full with specialists. The usual rollercoaster today after 2 good days, drama with the trachy resulted in a trachy change 16 days early, but I guess, now it should be a month before the next change. Looking forward to smooth sailing tomorrow! Take care XO

**17.01.16   Day 49        Week 7**

Good evening all, Samuel's had a busy week, the usual roller coaster ride. Pneumonia diagnosed today, a cannula inserted for a few days of iv antibiotics and blood testing. Finally some better ventilator settings have allowed Samuel to be comfortable with the ventilator for a few days. His new portable ventilator is due this week. Hope the settings are sorted quickly. Has had cuff down at his request for a while today so he had spoken with us. Saturday was Samuel's 'I've had enough' day, he was very out of sorts...to be expected though. Thankfully today has been a happier day. Now we look forward to some more improvements no matter how small, like the tiny left side of neck tensing we saw this last week. Have a good week, XO

**24.01.16   Day 56 Week 8**

As our 8th week is finishing, we continue to be thankful for the love, support and prayers from our family and friends (and others around the world). Samuel continues to lead the way for us with his bravery. This week's win was the catheter being removed & not being re-inserted! Hooray! He has been busy with specialists. Chest is much better, ventilator settings perfect, new vent arrived but won't use until chest is right, reached 27 degrees on tilt table...hope to break this record this week. Big things this week...a haircut ! Will be a tricky process:) Also going to trial swallowing ...a positive result might enable him to eat some thick food like custard. Has a new bed that can convert into a chair. Have a good week, XO

### 31.01.16   Day 63 Week 9

End of a busy week that saw Samuel with a neat haircut, clearer chest, a new ventilator that provided 36hrs of anxiety for Samuel (now settled), a new tilt table record of 48 degrees, & no swallow test until next week. He had the usual specialists working him hard. Had a turn on the cycle machine for his arms as well as his legs (at different times) which was nice to see. Won a quiz about India on Starlight tv:) some fun in the day! Underwent Motor Evoked Potential (anaethetised) to test motor pathways from brain to muscles—results showed what we have already seen body do. Also saw a very tiny flicker in left arm:), nothing in his right arm. Early days still, so praying for many more improvements, esp. in breathing. Have a safe and happy week. XO

### 01.02.16   Day 64

This is a happy Amelia moment to share. Amelia found out today she has been accepted into the Honours program at Griffith Uni and has gained a $24000 scholarship paid in part each semester. We are thrilled for her and proud of her achievements! Very thankful to our hospital Social Worker who assisted us to submit documents in order to request special consideration for Amelia's late application to be accepted. Thankfully, they agreed and she was given an equal chance with all other applicants. A good news story! XO

### 07.02.16   Week 10

Day 70 As Samuel is very comfortable on ventilator, cuff is down all day enabling him to speak. Often blinks responses, a habit more than necessity now. Trialling a dry circuit for couple of hours/day (usually on humidified one), so we can move around hospital more easily...and eventually out of the hospital. We have all commenced trachy training so we can do more to help Samuel in this area. Samuel asked a hypothetical question this week that allowed us to answer sharing some significant info about the motor pathways as they are at present as mentioned in our last message. This was pretty confronting for Samuel. Like us, he has not lost any hope though. Pretty determined to work hard. Tilt table reached 60 degrees for 42mins.

Leg cycling reached 6.07km in 40 mins and arm cycling reached 1.28km. Blue dye swallow test was successful so tomorrow the blue dye water test will happen...maybe food or beverage after that?? (Or maybe there's another blue dye test we don't know about yet:) Samuel's tape around his neck that holds the Trachy tube in place has been replaced with a chain that won't require daily changing like the tapes. We took an excursion to garden on level 5 on a drizzly day. Samuel asked to touch the plants as he hadn't touched anything for so long. School lessons at 11am this week....wonder what that will look like? Have a great week, and stay safe XO

### 15.02.16 Week 11

Samuel had a busy week, working hard as usual. Blue water testing continues, half tsp one day, 2 tsp another day, now to work up to 5 tsp. Each test involves 12 hrs of suctioning in his trachy tube at set intervals to make sure no blue comes up through the trachea. His left foot and leg have a little more movement. Cannula inserted for IV line for 2 doses of immuno haemoglobin (someone else's good blood), and trachy tube changed to the cuffless tube. All well with both processes. Setback on Friday with partial lung collapses causing problems with breathing and ventilation. Back on original vent as his new vent is not able to cater to sick lungs. This has caused a deal of worry for Samuel and loads of painful physio. Hopefully this will be quickly healed and we move forward again. Needless to say this wasn't the happiest of weekends for Samuel. Thankfully, today's a new day! Take care XO

### 21.02.16 Week 12

Day 84 done & dusted! Apologies if sms didn't get thru last week... tech issue:) or maybe just the user? Rough start to week with chest, but seems much better now & back on mobile vent—good. Drs identified factors contributing to lung issue—plans put in place to hopefully stop this happening again. Working hard at legs/moving-cycling, tilt table with Physio, OT working arms/hands cycling and ranging, passed 5 tsp blue water swallow test with Speech therapists...more to come...i, loved music therapy & Dexter dog visiting. Highlight of week—wearing school uniform while 2 friends visited with his teacher from school. 2 friends & a staff member aim to visit each week—wonderful for Samuel to have that connection. Hope all is well for you. Take care Blessings XO.

**28.02.16   Week 13**

What a week! A good week! Samuel's new wheels...a power wheelchair, controlled by his right foot was one of the highlights this week. He licked a lollipop and had a tasty swallow. His delight as he tasted this after nothing for 3 months was priceless. Samuel reached 75 degrees for 1 min & 71 degrees for 35 mins on tilt table. Determination plus. Samuel's leg movement continues to slowly increase much to his delight. Music therapy saw the completion of a composition of the song 'Radioactive'. As you can tell, he's worked really hard! Along with these good achievements, & many other activities, there were many challenges in the week. All tackled head on! His food has been changed to hopefully increase his weight by half to 1 kg a week. Hope u too have had a good week. Take care, XO

**06.03.16   Week 14**

Day 98... challenging week—chest issues with lower lung collapse still, and back on to old non portable ventilator again to deal with his troublesome lungs. Unscheduled Trachy change to a cuffed one so cuff can be up at night to help re-inflate lungs. So far it is down during day so can talk. Swallowing on hold until he has an xray to show if all is good while swallowing a special dye. A concern with swallow, after water came out his nose. Not been able to get out and about in power chair due to vent change. Still been a busy therapy week, but has needed more rests along the way. Highlight was ceasing a painful nightly injection after 3 months of this and a month of morning injections. Yahoo! Samuel's jaw seems to have clicked back almost into alignment which has helped his speech become clearer. A weight increase of .6kg which is good. Not our best week overall, but hope the week ahead will be a better one leading to healthy lungs. Have a good week, Blessings XO

**13.03.16   Week 15**

Week 15 over. Samuel received award from school this week for 'trying his best at all times'. Typifies his attitude to all he does each day. His timetable—very full with all teams working to get him to the best he can get. Day 100 Samuel had a visit from 2 Broncos players—highlight of his week. They were wonderful & chatted with him easily. Cuff is up at all times now, so no/limited speech, while the lungs recuperate. Chest Physio has him using a 'cough assist' machine twice daily for 15mins a time... way faster and less painful than 90 mins of chest beating Physio twice a day. Unfortunately Craig's mum (down from Hervey Bay) fell in a pothole on way to hospital to see Samuel, in hospital for 6wks with compound fracture of ankle. Take care XO

**14.03.16  Day 106**

A link we wanted to share. Broncos Make Surprise Visit—Broncos www.broncos.com.au/ news/2016/03/09/broncos-make-surprise-visit/ Didn't see this until tonight. The visit made his day last week! XO

*Bronco's visit, 9 March 2016*

**20.03.16  Week 16**

Another busy week in bed 3. Samuel's lungs are a little better, cuff remains up all night & most of day. Antibiotics now to help lungs too. Back on portable vent... to try to stop drs changing settings Respiratory Dr has set for lungs to improve. High blood pressure causing concern, too much calcium (leeching from bones) in blood and urine. Specialists working on correcting these concerns. The eye gaze has arrived :) & learning about its use has started again. Typifying Samuel, he said to us tonight, 'there's something I've been meaning to say for a while, I should have told you before but I need to tell you now. Thank you for loving and supporting me for all this time.' One in a million this boy! Have a great week. Blessings XO

**27.03.16  Week 17**

Happy Easter! What a good but busy week Samuel has had. After 114 days, Samuel had a shower in his shower chair. Loved the water pouring over his body. A few minor improvements needed on this chair. Special visit last Monday by Olympic swimmers Bronte and Cate Campbell. Lungs seem to be clearing, calcium levels being lowered, blood pressure lowered, hair was cut, & wheelchair driving improving.

Has given his music therapist a cello lesson:) Eye gaze being used for short periods of time...many programs going to be included on this device. FYI Craig's mum who has a compound fracture of her ankle, (happened 200m from hospital, on route from Hervey Bay) to visit Samuel 2 weeks ago, suffered a stroke on Wednesday. (While in PA hospital.) Blessings XO

**03.04.16   Week 18**

Samuel has been busy wheelchair manoevering around PICU and level 2...keen to get his licence from the physio. He's been down on a mat & been rolled and stretched with Physio's help. Trachy changes remain too tight, so surgery is likely to correct some granulation inside stoma. Gastro team working towards changing feeding tube in nose to one direct into stomach PEG. This journey continues with it's neverending procedures. Met a black Labrador named Chilli this week who received a strong foot pat from Samuel. A shower is planned for Wednesday, in the modified chair... hopefully an even better experience. Samuel continues to be positive in his attitude towards his improvement. Have a happy week. XO

**10.04.16   Week 19**

Samuel's highlight last Sat. was going to the 14th floor doors to check our the helipad. Fabulous view! How did we forget to share that? Samuel has been keeping Drs & nurses updated on what procedures he has coming up...asking questions of staff if we r not with him:) Sadly we r not there early in the morning when some make their rounds...he's keeping them in check:) Fluroscopy showed good control of liquid in his mouth, but he's not getting the swallow action happening. Another challenge we pray will be overcome with time and effort. Dexter's visit was good therapy this week. Dentist visited to extract a baby molar that's been struggling to come out for months... Loosened it with his tongue, then helped him wiggle it out .. 8 mins before dentist arrived..perfect timing. An amazing half hour excursion—walk/drive across 2 roads & about 100m up the footpath towards Grey St (South Bank) in the outside world... great feeling after 131 days on hospital premises!  Doing some great driving and learning wheelchair etiquette! Yesterday Samuel celebrated his 10th birthday (early) on the PICU balcony with lots of family and a few friends. A great occasion for Samuel to celebrate with some of the wonderful people praying for him and loving him unconditionally. Blessings to all for the week ahead! XO

### 17.04.16   Week 20

Day 140 finishes a busy, with some fun-filled times week. Samuel had a great birthday heading to South Bank driving his wheelchair—ventilator attached. He enjoyed the bit of freedom, with us, special friends & 2 nurses close by. Samuel & special friend Olivia spent quality 'kid' time watching & feeding a bearded dragon in garden. Simply beautiful to see! Therapies kept him moving—arm & leg cycling, tilt table, mat work, mouth & tongue exercises, & limb ranging. School at hosp changing, look at attending the hosp school for 1hr on 1+ days. Big week ahead—3 procedures under 1 general anaesthetic. Craig coped with the week back at work & I survived hospital on my own until Craig came in after work. Hoping we (you & us) all gave a good week ahead. XO

### 20.04.16   Day 143

Dear Family and Friends, in my life I have been one to make sure I do things like 'saying thank you' perfectly and timely. I have come to realise these past months, that I can't physically do this the way I want to. So apologies in advance for this message not being personalised. By sharing this message with you, I will (hopefully) be able to acknowledge to myself, I have done what I needed to do to say 'thank you'. Over the last months you may have done one or more very kind acts for Samuel & our family—be it visiting, gifting money for parking, providing meals, providing gift vouchers, celebrating Samuel's birthday on the balcony, gifts for Samuel, helping cater for Samuel's party or other acts that escape my mind at present. We appreciate and are so thankful for all of the incredible support we have received and continue to receive. Thank you, thank you, thank you!! Much love and blessings XOXO Jane, Craig, Amelia & Samuel

### 24.04.16  Week 21

Oh my, what a massive week. Surgery saw the feeding PEG inserted-this will remain long term for feeding as further investigations show Samuel has no muscles working to make a swallow. The tracheostomy surgery went well, a larger tube was inserted after the stoma was cleaned up inside & widened. The bronchoscopy cleared a few plugs from his lungs that didn't look too bad. Unfortunately the epiglottis is not moving at all which places Samuel's lungs at risk of infection should any fluid/food/saliva go into them accidentally. Respiratory Dr instructed the cuff on his trachy tube be put up indefinitely—which means he has lost his voice. This is tough, as his vocal cords (assessed in theatre before surgery began) are actually working —now he can't use them. After receiving that news from specialists, we & the wider medical team decided Samuel needed to know more info about his prognosis. In addition to the above information, Samuel is now aware (although said he was already aware of most of this info) he is on long term ventilation as his diaphragm is paralysed, his hands & arms will not regain movement. As u can imagine, many tears have been shed over last few days. At the end of the gloomy part of our talk with Samuel, an equally brave Amelia went through a long list we had made of good things about Samuel—what he can do, what is working well and identified many of his fabulous traits that make our brave Samuel the person that he is. To give an idea of time in hospital, we pray we are home before Christmas. Huge .... absolutely! Even though all this is sounding pretty gloomy, we have by no means given up hope that our Drs currently researching/ a miracle/ or medical break-through in the years ahead might just happen to improve these current outcomes. Looking forward, Samuel's week ahead has him back on track with therapists...& hopefully not so much screen time:) Guess we did have to let him get over the pain from this week's procedures...stomach in particular is very tender. Thank you for your continued love, support & prayers. May the week ahead be a happy one for all. XO

**01.05.06   Week 22**

Dear family and friends, this week Samuel spent a lot of time in bed due to stomach pain...bowels taking their time to get back in action after surgery and an infection in the PEG site causing swelling and loads of pain. Cannula inserted promptly for IV antibiotics. Site looking much better. Samuel has felt much better since Thursday thankfully. No trachy tube change was Samuel's favourite for the week. Samuel has enjoyed being independent in the wheelchair (with ventilator on the back) these last few days, especially greeting some visitors at the doors to PICU. Samuel has surgery again on the trachy site this week. Hopefully all is looking good, and then no more surgery for 10 weeks. Have a happy week:) XO

**08.05.16   Week 23**

Day 161 Samuel has had some great social catch ups—nice to see him enjoying company of other people. The tracheostomy surgery went well. Thankfully not too much discomfort afterwards. Samuel visited the hospital school to meet classmates. Aim is to go to this school for 1 hr, 1-3 times a week, in weeks ahead. We had 2 impromptu outings this week, across the road to coffee shop, and out to lunch at Zambreros. Tough not to eat same food as us, but his feed was going through at same time:) Being out of the hospital was brilliant! Always must be 2 vent and trachy trained people with Samuel to leave PICU front doors. We love it when a nurse becomes available to join us to escape. Happy Mothers' Day to all Mums! Have a happy week, XO

**15.05.16   Week 24**

24 weeks—Samuel faced some challenges but had some enjoyment too. Trachy change went well, managed without meds &remained calm. After 21 weeks being anxious about trachy changes & 13 traumatic changes, I think we have finally hit the jackpot! Soon WE will be changing these tubes instead of drs/nurses. Samuel did 2 of 4 Naplan tests, was visited by a Virgin Airline pilot, saw 2 tiger cubs, did his usual therapies, enjoyed visitors & escaped to South Bank with 2 nurses(twice). Craig & I returned from a meeting about media & funding to find a note on the bed—'escaped to South Bank Lagoon, see ya round.' We caught up with him. Believe he was happy to be

out joking with the nurses without us in tow. Hope to attend school on level 8 this week... see how we go. Beginning to trial speech devices. Have a happy week. XO

**22.05.16 (sent 23.05.16)    Week 25**

Week 25 Samuel enjoyed 2 sessions at school this week, aiming for the same next week. Escaped level 4 to go to South Bank, around the hospital block, & a nurses' coffee run across the road. Found out our house can be modified to cater to Samuel's needs. For that we are thankful. We started ventilator training :) QLD Health team filmed & interviewed Samuel using the eye gaze, for an ehealth award. Visitors including Broncos—Jack Reid & Lachlan Maranta, therapies, showers, all helped to fill our days. Started 'Campaign for Samuel'. A lot of great steps taken towards getting home. Not enjoying trying to use speech devices-with practice it should become easier. Major hiccup to end our week—burst pipe in ensuite flooding whole house. May week ahead be a good one!

**28.05.16   Day 181**

A short message to share..tomorrow's *Brisbane Sunday Mail* should have an article about Samuel in the paper. If u can't access this paper in person, the Courier/Sunday Mail will have the article available online—unblocked so non'subscribets can see it.  Hoping this generates more interest in Samuel's cause. XO

**29.05.16   Week 26**

What a huge week. 26 weeks! Trialled or viewed some items we need for when we venture home. Most items we need to view/trial 3 samples so we choose the items best suited to Samuel. Some big achievements...2 taxi rides (after being keen for his 1st trip, he was quite emotional and thought he couldn't do it...but in true Samuel style after a lot of encouragement, he said, 'Go on, just do it'...and he enjoyed it), & seeing Angry Birds movie at cinemas. Usual therapy & school once due to staffing. I performed my first trachy change, so progress on that front. Going to be 2 changes each week until we are all trained. Craig & Amelia to perform these in weeks ahead. Had week out of house while it dried, but back home now. Have a great week! XO

**05.06.16   Week 27**

Day 189 Hello, Hoping you saw the respectful *Sunday Mail* article last week. Samuel has had a reasonable week, kept busy with more equipment trials, vehicle modifications info, a half hour taxi ride, 2 hospital school visits & his usual therapies. Samuel's ventilation was a challenge this week. Has been over-ventilated for months to get him 'well' but now settings are being reduced slowly to a level that won't over-inflate his lungs & cause potential long term damage. Very challenging to hear him say he can't get enough breath. He is brave & working through tough times. I completed 2 trachy changes, Craig's turn now. Very thankful for those who r hosting events or planning long term strategy to raise funds for Samuel. Together we will get him home! Take care XO

**12.06.16   Week 28**

28 weeks A mixed bag this week, a few challenges but we worked through them. Friday finished with a bang...an x-ray revealed lungs look great, $CO_2$ levels good & vent settings stable:) A short visit to Samuel's SRSS to check out access for his power chair. Was to be a secret planning visit only known about by admin, but not secret once spotted on site. Samuel was very happy to see his school, some students & staff again after 6 long months. Samuel's tolerance of a speaking valve (that someone else has to occlude) has increased; it is so nice to hear his voice at times. I was given permission to be 2nd person for school/in hospital outings :) Vent training will get us out of the hospital for trips...we r working on that! Attended hospital school twice this week. He enjoys seeing his hospital class mates. Had a computer face to face link up with his SRSS school class this week, hoping to join in some lessons in the near future. Craig completed 2nd trachy tube change, one to go to be competent! Amelia's turn soon—once her exams are over. The support 'Campaign for Samuel' is receiving is truly amazing! Thank you for sharing. Have a great week! XO

**19.06.16   Week 29**

Day 203 Medication weaning is causing a bit of dizziness & headaches this week. We test drove a Kia Carnival modified for a wheelchair with

Samuel in it. Was a much smoother ride for Samuel than being in a Maxi Taxi. Craig is now trachy competent, & we had another vent training session. Samuel worked well in his usual therapy sessions. Music therapy was a hit this week. Samuel was able to kick his football from his bed with his right leg hanging over the side with the aim to have it land on a bass drum, the bongo drums or the tambourine...trying to keep to a beat. The music therapist had a great workout & Samuel thoroughly enjoyed this activity. A big week ahead, starting with attending a whole school parade on Monday morning. Exciting! Take care. XO

**26.06.16   Week 30**

30 weeks today... Samuel's visit to school on Monday was fantastic. He was so excited to see and be with his friends & school staff. If you search Albert & Logan Newspapers you should find an article about this visit & a picture of him with 2 friends. Had more home modifications talks this week. A little bit of voice is coming around trachy cuff— praying this isn't allowing secretions into his lungs and compromising their 'good' status. Quieter 2 weeks ahead therapy wise—aim to get out & about more ... as it is holidays after all! Channel 9 news visited last week, story should air this week. Will text when, once known. Still some unsettled nights with medication weaning, but improving. Blessings for the week ahead. XO

**29.06.16   Day 213**

Heads up...not our news story filmed last week, but Ch 9 news were at Samuel's school this morning interviewing Principal about election day BBQ fundraising for Samuel while a mock BBQ was thrown together for filming..... This goes to air tonight. Reckon next week for Samuel's story. XO

**03.07.16   Week 31**

Dear family & friends, not much therapy for Samuel this week. Medically things r going well. Monday saw me signed off on vent training & allowed to be 2nd trained person for outings—so with our nurse we can more easily escape PICU bed 3. We have been to South Bank vacinity about

3 times, across Good Will Bridge & back, to the movies, to Samuel's school on election day (bbq & bake stall raising $ for Samuel) for a short but very supportive visit & out to a business which shows 'smart switches' to see what is available to Samuel. Actually has been a huge week—haven't had this much fresh air in about 7 months! If u missed it, Ch 9 link to story aired tonight—Craig will add to social media. Looking forward to another holiday week ahead:) Blessings to all XO

**10.07.16   Week 32**

Week 32 ...my how time is just going. Another fun week of school holidays with a little bit of challenging therapy. Caught up with some family & friends during the week, saw 2 movies, walked through South Bank...& the markets, visited Dymocks bookshop & celebrated Amelia's 18th birthday at a restaurant for lunch. Still have a little voice coming through, but an x-ray has shown the lungs still look good...hooray! A busier week ahead:) Hope u enjoy your week & we'll aim to enjoy ours! Much love. XOx

**11.07.16   Day 225**

Evening, couldn't keep this for the end of the week...sorry NSW supporters, Go QLD! Samuel received a surprise visit from his NRL favourite Sam Thaiday. Also visited by Greg Inglis GI & Nate Myles who called in on the way to the airport to head to Melbourne for State of Origin. All 3 were amazing with Samuel. Will send a second photo shortly. A happy start to the week...after 3 hours at hospital school:) blessings XO

**17.07.16   Week 33**

Week 33, what a huge one it's been. Samuel was visited by—3 Maroons' players including Sam Thaiday his NRL favourite; a very amazing Taylor Swift; 2 Broncos including Ben Hunt; and to finish his week—2 Paralympic basketballers one of whom had Transverse Myelitis at age 18. These 2 positive men spoke openly with Samuel ...great role models! School attendance is increasing, but not full days as therapy sessions r still very important. Trialling equip't continues to make sure we get what's right for Samuel's needs. Thankfully a haircut today has him neat & tidy again. Cuff pressures on trachy tube have been reduced slightly allowing a little more forced voice, hopefully not compromising lungs. 'Ghostbusters' movie was enjoyed today. Have a happy week! XO

**20.07.16   Day 234**

Dear Samuel supporters, a Campaign for Samuel t-shirt print run is looking possible. Some of you have said you would like a shirt. If you would like to purchase a shirt $25 each, pls let me know and I'll forward details on how to pay, indicate shirt size and have your name on the order. If u r part of a group (eg school), perhaps one of you could be the contact person for your group? Might make it easier to get shirts to you too. Size wise, Amelia has an M which is a tad big on her. Craig's is 2XL, Jane's 3XL and very long and Samuel's is a Small (and big on him) sizes available S, M, L, XL, 2XL, 3XL 4XL. No pressure at all. just offering as we need 20 for min. order. My cousin & her son are running in Bridge 2 Brisbane raising funds for Samuel and awareness of the campaign. XO PLS make contact by 8pm Friday, details will then be forwarded by Saturday night so order/payment can be placed ASAP. Cut of time for payment will be Wed 27th. Have a great day! XO Thornes

**24.07.16   Week 34**

Week 34 saw Samuel attend school every day for 2 sessions most days. Physio tested Samuel with his time on the tilt table stretching out his muscles. OT, speech & music therapy continued. Ultrasound done on liver, but all looks good. Calcium levels creeping up so Renal team will assess. A relaxing weekend—saw movie 'Hunt for the Wilderpeople' and chased Pokemon at South Bank with 1000s of other chasers. No celebrities this week, just good old fashioned friends! Have a great week. XO

**31.07.16   Week 35**

Oh my the weeks are rolling by. Number 35 Phew! Samuel had a big school week, minimum 2 sessions each day. A whole day there knocked him a bit. Received an award on parade.. as above :) Outside school sessions— he had his usual therapies. Busy! Equipment trials continue. Found a bed he finds very comfortable & can move himself using a scanner with a button. Week ahead holds the usual therapy, school work, a visit from Perry Cross a ventilated quadriplegic and hopefully an easy general anaesthetic for surgery on Tuesday morning to change gastroscopy peg (30cm of tubing) to a MicKey (more like a button) for feeding direct to stomach. Hoping you have had a good week! We continue to be thankful for the wonderfully supportive family and friends we have been blessed with. Take care. XO

### 07.08.16   Week 36

Week 36 has been huge. School, therapies, dietician made changes to diet & Ekka fun day at hospital. Visit from Perry Cross was inspirational—he's happy to catch up with Samuel again in future & to answer Samuel's questions. Surgery went well, although beforehand was quiet stressful for Samuel. Any further surgeries will involve pre-meds to ease anxiety. New feeding MicKey button is going well & caused limited pain after surgery. Amelia performed her 1st trache change, both she & Samuel did well:) Very proud of her...it really is a challenge! Best news for week is something we have been waiting to hear—the approval has been granted for funding for carers & home ventilation for Samuel. This will progress through a process with 'Mater at Home' who employ carers and train them according to Samuel's needs. Very blessed for this decision as it has taken some families 1-3 years for this to happen. Some additional funding has been approved so we do not have as many out of pocket expenses for essential medical equipment. We r yet to see this list. Amazing! We will continue to raise funds for equipment not funded, our modified vehicle & of course our house modifications. Slowly but surely our progress to going home continues. Christmas at home might just be a reality & not a dream. Another busy week ahead—the highlight will hopefully be a visit to home on Wednesday. Enjoy your week:) Blessings, XO

### 15.08.16   Week 37

Good morning, week 37 saw Samuel enjoy 2 visits to home. It was so nice to have us all in our own home spending time together. We had a nurse accompany us each time & they blended in & tried to be very unobtrusive. Samuel is enjoying school & working well in class...not the chatterbox he used to be at school. Pretty good set up with a teacher & an aide for his Yr 5/6 class which last week had 3 & 4 students each day. He still managed his therapies & more equipment trials. Another busy week ahead—praying it's a good one for us and for you too. Take care, XO

### 22.08.16   Week 38

Day 266 was a quiet one. This week included school excursions to the LCCH Medical research building & the Sciencentre. Had a short visit home & a lovely morning with the Broncos after training. Samuel spoke to many players, Wayne Bennett & Wally Lewis. Was particularly special when Sam Thaiday saw Samuel & called out 'Hey Sammy boy'! Weaning has commenced on blood pressure meds with no change to BP which is good. He spent a night at the sleep/respiratory study. Outcome—vent settings can be reduced further which is better for his lungs. He only slept for 6 hours so Melatonin will continue to be given to help regulate his sleep patterns. Last 24hrs there has been a minor problem with Samuel's lungs with a little fluid build-up, but not pneumonia so that's a blessing. Praying this is sorted ASAP. Craig fielded a 20min phone call from the Minister for Health to talk about Samuel. We hope Samuel will be able to meet the Health Minister. Another busy week ahead...hope it's a good one for all! Take care. XO

### 28.08.16   Week 39

Week 39 done & dusted. Thankfully Samuel's lungs have improved. This has been a busy week with school, therapies, & completing funding applications. Trachy change was done by ENT nurse & Dr as concerns with stoma site. Going to monitor 4 next few weeks... if improved—great, if not—more surgery to tidy up inside site again. Hospital launched revised values on Friday & Craig spoke on our behalf on the value of Care as requested by hospital administration. Exciting news is our KIA Carnival is on its way to Sydney for modifications—should mean it's back earlier than Christmas as was originally thought. We ventured out to watch some powerchair soccer, but not sure exactly about Samuel's thoughts. He didn't say much—maybe it was a bit overwhelming? Another big week ahead for our family. Take care. XO

### 04.09.16   Week 40

Week 40 Starting to feel like we have been here forever, staying positive though, as every day is another day closer to home. Had a very quiet weekend in, after a big week out & about. Visited Samuel's school on Tues night for the annual Variety Night-great to be there with the faces we love to see. Wed Craig went on hosp school trip to Newstead House with Samuel. Thurs enjoyed lunch at South Bank & a fabulous night at the Broncos...in the tunnels under Suncorp Stadium, out on to the turf, down to the Diamond Lounge viewing room where we could see players warming up. Highlight of course was meeting up with some familiar faces and the Broncos winning. Oh yes, managed to fit in school & therapies too :) Happy Fathers' Day to all the Dads! Take care, XO

### 11.09.16   Week 41

287 days down...The highlight of the week was Samuel & Amelia each receiving a 'Certificate of Courage' award from the Lions Club with a number of family & friends in attendance. Samuel has worked on therapies & attended school each day. The tilt table caused some pain in lower legs, so wearing ankle/foot orthotics in bed each night to help stretch out the muscles & keep correct foot position. Ventilator pressures reduced to 'new' normal with no stress to Samuel. Developing a reliance on Cough Assist machine, so working with him to reduce anxiety about secretions he can feel in his chest—tough on us all. Bed for home...ordered. Trial of tailor—made shower chair should be this week. All progress on the road to home. Nearly school holidays :) Blessings XO

### 18.09.16   Week 42

Week 42 Samuel had a busy week completing school work tasks, painting with his foot a Sidney Nolan's scene from Ned Kelly series. The teacher was amazing with Samuel who was so proud of his finished work. Samuel donated some table tennis paddles to the school much to his friends' delight—after discussing this with the Principal. We are very proud of him wanting to do something for others. Samuel's trachy change was a challenge, but the stoma will be assessed again in 4 wks. There was a slight improvement in the tracheal granulation, hoping for this to continue. Therapies continued as did unsuccessful shower chair & hoist trials—seems Samuel's body is a challenge. Very pleased to see him 'gobble up' the book The 78 Storey Treehouse'...sometimes struggles to find his love of reading when not able to turn pages himself. He's not keen on a kindle but will keep working on this. Today he beat us (convincingly) at Monopoly, much to our disgust:) We hope to have a few activities outside hospital this week. Have a great week ahead. Take care, XO

### 25.09.16   Week 43

Day 301 yesterday ended a quiet week of school holidays. Last week Samuel had a few therapy sessions, trips to movies & a Monopoly morning. He had blue dye tests for liquids again that showed he has good control of liquid in his mouth so is again allowed to taste and have liquid suctioned out. He has been nominated for Pride of Aust. medal—pg 32 of Sunday Mail. Proud...yes! We celebrated day 300 with fireworks overlooking the Brisbane River. We are looking forward to another week of school holidays. Have a great week, XO

### 02.10.16   Week 44

A mixed week for us. Craig & I spent most mornings at home packing and sorting, while Samuel had speech, OT and Physio therapy sessions before some 'free time, which means internet time:) We filled our afternoons together catching up with Sam Thaiday, having a pleasant meeting with the Minister for Health, playing board games, going to the movies and meeting up with some friends. Highlight for weekend was heading home for a few hours, where Samuel helped make some decisions on the many toys in the house. Have a great week, XO

### 09.10.16   Week 45

Week 45 Mixed emotions week from a high of attending a fantastic Trivia & Auction night run by Campaign 4 Samuel fundraising group at Samuel's school. May make this an annual event! The low was moving to room 10, half the size, but still all the equipment has to fit in. This has been an adjustment for us all, especially Samuel. His old room was able to be pressurized—used mainly by cancer patients. Lucky to have the 'PICU penthouse' for 9.5 months :) Another reason to be discharged ASAP:) Still hoping for before Xmas... fingers crossed. Samuel had lots of school & enjoyed being back with the class. Trachy was changed a week earlier than planned—ENT staff not able view the site next week. I did the change, ENT checked the site & thankfully all looked improved, so surgery should be off the radar. Take care, XO

### 16.10.16    Week 46

Week 46 Samuel continues to stay well. He's coping with his room and the associated moving of furniture as we move him from bed to chair etc. We have to go to Rehab ward for tilt table now as there is no way it could be done in this smaller room. We enjoyed a day at home on Saturday. Another busy week ahead with school, therapies and yet another shower chair trial. Have a great week, we sure aim to. XO

### 23.10.16    Week 47

Week 47 has been another busy week. Samuel was proud to deliver the 'Acknowledgement to Country' on the Pupil free day to 80 Ed QLD staff from hospital, Metro East schools & the DG of Education. We struck gold with our shower chair trial—only took 5 trials to find a comfortable one... so pleased we found it! Progress! School & therapies filled Samuel's days. Samuel endured a painful spine xray experience to ascertain whether there is any curving which sadly is inevitable. It will also be useful to compare when next xray is taken in the future. We all enjoyed a relaxing day at home yesterday. We were excited to hear this week our modified car should be ready in early Nov. not Dec. Hoping we hear about house mods starting soon. Have a good week. XO

### 30.10.16    Week 48

Week 48 included all the usual therapies and school. Samuel tasted a vanilla milkshake with ice-cream mixed in, thicker shake to be tasted this week in lead up to ice-cream. Samuel spent Thursday morning at Springwood

Rd SS which he really enjoyed. The school was well prepared for his visit and in true Samuel style he just took the visit in his stride. I believe he was thinking, well this is my school, no big deal. Expressed he wants to stay for longer next time:) We had a wonderful day at home on Saturday, these days for us are a nice treat after a long, busy hospital week. Hope the carers we are given are as nice as the nurses who come home with us for these visits. Have a happy week ahead. Blessings, XO

**06.11.16   Week 49**

Week 49  Our weeks are filled much the same these days... Therapies, school, and a day at home on the weekend. Just to clarify, when Samuel tastes drinks and any future food, it is purely for tasting, and then suctioning/removing from his mouth. He is still not able to swallow.  No car in our possession yet, but maybe by the end of the week.  The Nerf gun mounted on Samuel's chair has had a workout the last 2 Sundays. Good fun! Have a good week, take care. XO

**09.11.16   Extra message**

Dear family & friends

Many people have been working to support us and Samuel in many ways. Thanks. I would like to let you know of other 'behind-the-scenes' developments from over the last few months.

The incorporated association Campaign for Samuel Inc. was established (there will be more info soon about memberships and joining). Sanction to fundraise for an indefinite period has been approved by the Office of Fair Trading. Establishment of the 'Samuel Thorne Fund'—a tax deductible, not-for-profit public fund. Registration of the domain campaignforsamuel.org. au (redirects to our initial/temporary website). Creation of a 'GiveNow. com.au' account for the Samuel Thorne Fund—this will allow the closure of the GoFundMe account: GiveNow passes on 100% of donations for bank transfers and takes a small percentage for Visa & Mastercard transactions. There is no charge for regular, automated monthly bank transfers. (We are still setting up receipting capability for manual donations so would prefer at this stage for donations to go through GiveNow).

What does all this mean? We are now, finally in a position to receive tax deductible donations for the fund and hopefully increase the donations from the corporate/business sector. From the first official campaign meeting to this point has taken just 70 days. I'm pretty proud of how quickly this has been achieved. Love to all XO, Craig

**13.11.16   Week 50**

Week 50 has been busy, busy! Samuel has enjoyed the nurses this week scoring a couple of his favourites, some weeks there r more new faces than familiar ones. To have his 'favourites' makes for nicer days for Samuel. Samuel had a visit to Springwood Road School for 3 & half hrs, and thoroughly enjoyed himself. Another visit is planned for 1st Dec. Craig's text during the week although maybe a little late at night for some, was great to share this accomplishment. We are still waiting on the car to be ready ... playing the 'hopefully next week' game. Best news this week was plans are back from council, so maybe now we'll have some mods start one day soon. We had a great day home yesterday despite an electrical storm. Samuel may appear briefly on Channel 9 Today Show at 7:12am on Friday morning when they cross for the weather to the hospital school promoting the Children's Foundation Telethon. Amelia has finished Uni exams, next her vent training. She has 3rd trachy change to go next week, forgot to mention last week she had done her 2nd one. Have a happy week, XO

**20.11.16   Week 51**

Day 357 who would have thought we would be here this long? Best news for week ahead is work commencing on building Amelia's room. Sadly our house won't be ready for Christmas, maybe February at this stage. Car... maybe this week? Hopefully our trip in a maxi taxi today was last one?? Had a lovely day at home today. Was a good week at school. Samuel visited our family dentist which thankfully was a good experience. Only 3 baby teeth left :) Have a happy and safe week. XO

**27.11.16   Week 52**

Day 364 Week 52 done & dusted. Feeling rather heavy-hearted & fragile reflecting on this Sunday night last year...our trip to Logan emergency resulting in admission to Lady Cilento Hospital where our beautiful boy remains ... for now. Like every hurdle to date we will move on with our marathon. On a happy note, took delivery of our car on Friday. Samuel is very comfortable with the smoother ride & can see out in front of him. A docking plate will be fitted before too long & then the car will be complete. The slab for Amelia's room has been poured & the internal walls will go up this week. Samuel has one final assessment to complete at school, then he will have a relaxing last 2 weeks. Thank you for your prayers and support. Take care XO

### 04.12.16   Day 371

Week 53 Samuel thoroughly enjoyed a performance by 'Two Cellos' on the 30th...a much better way to spend that date. He organised with his teachers a 'thank you lunch' for some of the hospital staff who helped him on his journey this year. Beautiful! He slotted into a day at Springwood Road SS which went well. More visits home, & seeing the progress of the room being built for Amelia—wiring & insulation completed. Samuel joined us for a wider family Christmas gathering. In amongst all these activities, he attended school full time and squeezed in some therapy after school. Still trialling portable hoists—one last week & one tomorrow. Hoping it's a suitable one. Last week of Year 5 ahead for Samuel. Take care XO

### 11.12.16   Week 54

Day 378 Samuel has had a pretty easy week. Visited Springwood Road SS for their final school parade & was presented with a chq for $64000 from the fundraising his school has done over the last 6 months. A massive help that will be! Trial of portable hoist didn't strike gold. Biomedical engineers are now looking to see what can be done to sort out a hoist. Samuel had fun at school, some of his art work was used to make gift wrap, cards and gift tags. These items along with other items made by hospital school children were then sold at a stall. The profits are then donated to the Hospital Foundation & a charity as voted by the children. We finished our week off with 2 day trips to home on the weekend. Blessings to all, XO

**14.12.16**

Happy Wednesday, hope your day is going well. Just a heads up, Samuel's story will appear on Channel 7 news tonight at 6pm and a snippet on 4pm news. The emphasis for the story was on getting home for Christmas, and the tennis auction for the Australian Tennis Open. Let's hope it has an effect :) Bless you all. XO

**18.12.16**

Day 385 Samuel has had a quieter week without school. We enjoyed a drive home to collect Craig—that filled our time nicely. Starlight Captains challenged Samuel to a naming elements competition ...good fun for all ...Samuel won. Samuel enjoyed some Christmas festivities at hospital on level 2. Had a short trip to South Bank Geo Caching (like Pokemon Go, but real things to find). Speech Therapy tasting finally reached biting into an icy pole, chewing ice-cream, & Hubba Bubba gum. All were suctioned/ spat out, but he did enjoy all experiences! He caught up with Sam Thaiday at Starlight Christmas party. We had a 7 News story filmed & Courier Mail visited as Samuel is part of a kids in hospital at Christmas article. Xmas Eve paper—Insight section we think. Thoroughly enjoyed a night trip to see our friends' amazing Christmas lights display, something we used to do each year. Seeing Samuel's delight was special. Enjoyed a visit home on Saturday & drive through Brisbane's tunnels today. We are so very blessed to have had some very special (favourite) nurses accompany us on our outings. There are always nice, new nurses in PICU, but after 55 weeks we do have our favourites. Have a fabulous week, and a very Happy Christmas. XO

**25.12.16**

Day 392  Samuel enjoyed Fantastic Beasts & Trolls at cinemas. Pokemon catching with Amelia was favourite activity. Samuel had trache change which went smoothly. He is so much calmer, which is good when there's a lifetime ahead of these every 3-4 weeks. Amelia's ventilator training underway, soon be all trained & able to venture out with Samuel & the nurse. Also fitted in a few trips in the car, a haircut in salon, a successful portable hoist trial (yahoo!), patting reindeer, a few therapies, tasting tuna sushi &

teriyaki chicken, & taking delivery of shower commode ...more progress:)
House mods on break now, restart 9/1. Christmas Eve & Christmas Day
at home together without a nurse—was much hoop jumping through by
hospital administration to do this. Have a happy week. Take care, XO

### 2017

**01.01.17**

Day 399 (Sunday) Happy New Year! Samuel has had a happy week.
This week most days were spent at home—4 without our nurse. Usually
home by 10ish and back to hospital by 6ish. Samuel spends a lot of time
directing someone in XBox one games. He enjoyed 8:30pm fireworks
on NYE with friends. House wise, the container comes tomorrow then
to empty the house!  Boxes everywhere! Builders back on 9th January.
Getting closer to home every day. Have a great week! XO

**08.01.17   Week 58    Day 406**

Samuel has visited home every day this week. We have nearly completed
packing the contents of our house in preparation for more mods start this
week. 18.5 yrs accumulation of 'stuff' & 2 kids... 6m container is nearly
full. Kidney ultrasound this week shows improved kidney health, but also
a few small stones. Specialists to decide on plan for this. A little more neck
movement pulling to right noticed early this week. This may be another
way to control switches sometime in the future. Have a happy week. XO

**15.01.17   Week 59    Day 413**

Week 59 House modifications have started, the kitchen &
bathroom have been stripped, Samuel's bedroom walls and family/
lounge/office walls have been removed. Thankfully we were 'out' not
long after power was cut on Tuesday. We are now staying at Kangaroo
Point about 5mins from hospital. Samuel spent daytime at apartment
this weekend. A few therapies last week and a trip to the shops... EB
Games to find XBox games. Hope your week has been a good one. XO

**22.01.17   60 weeks    Day 420**

60 weeks  It has been quite a relaxing week for Samuel. Movies,
almost daily visits to the apartment, and entertainment by the Starlight

Captains. House demolition about finished, a bit of construction happening and lots of decision making around fixtures for bathroom, lighting and power points throughout house. Special day tomorrow as Samuel returns to his school, with the hospital school as the back-up plan if it becomes too much in these first few weeks. Exciting week ahead. All the best for your week. XO

**29.01.17   61 weeks     Day 427**

Week 61 saw Samuel at Springwood Road SS fulltime! He enjoyed his days, watching & catching up with his friends and getting ready for learning. He was very tired after school, but managed to push through. Australia Day and the weekend each gave the opportunity for an 8:30am wake up. This week we expect the MicKey feeding button will need changing. This will be the first one of these for us to be involved in. It's supposed to be easy & painless ... hopefully for all. House wise the tiles for wet rooms were chosen, hopefully more action on the house this week. Moved apartments (next door) on Friday night to a slightly larger apartment that accommodates Samuel better. Have a great week! XO

**05.02.17   62 weeks     Day 434**

Week 62 Samuel enjoyed school each day again this week. He had a minor medical challenge at school which was worked through & sorted out. Good to experience any issues while I am in classroom with Samuel these first 4-6 weeks of school while school staff is developing their skills & how comfortable they are with Samuel. A nurse currently comes with us each day, will be replaced by support worker/carer once discharged from hospital or closer to discharge. Samuel had his first 6 monthly MicKey feeding button changed. Was anxious before the change, however once done, was calm & feeling good. Ask him one day about the change & he might share a funny story. We are proud of Samuel nominating for school captain & delivering his speech. Have a happy week ahead. XO

**12.02.17   63 weeks     Day 441**

Day 441 Discharge is getting closer every day...hopefully home & settled before Easter. School week was a busy one, but Samuel coped well.

His teacher is a wonder making sure he is included or has a variation so he is completing necessary work. He also has 2 friendly & very switched on teacher aides who work with him during the day for all his educational needs. Samuel still has a team of school staff committed to ensuring Samuel needs are being met. We have met 8 experienced carers who will help provide 24/7 care at home & school, all attended training specific to Samuel's needs. Routine blood tests yesterday. House modifications are going well, great to see plans coming together slowly but surely. We are busy after school as hospital staff try to catch up with us. Take care XO.

**19.02.17    64 weeks    Day 448**

Week 64 Samuel started his week with an overnight sleep study. Showed $CO_2$ levels were too low during sleep so vent settings reduced to cater for this. No anxiety this time which is a relief. Samuel was not successful in gaining a leadership position, but we r very proud of his choice to have a go. He trialled his new power chair which is coming along nicely, more to be done still. Amelia did monthly trache change that went to plan. House mods saw ceiling hoist installed, and kitchen installed (no bench tops yet). Hospital teams associated with Samuel are working through all of the info & training needed for discharge. Samuel helped do grocery shopping this week. Think he enjoyed the challenge of finding the items on his list. Have a good week, we aim to! XO

**26.02.17    65 weeks    Day 455**

Day 455 ... Samuel had a good week full of schooling except for an afternoon at hospital school as Craig & I had a meeting at hospital. Samuel had a renal ultrasound to check on kidneys & their stones. No results as yet. Surgery booked for 8th March for lungs, tracheostomy stoma and trachea. House mods continue to chug along. Builders should be finished inside on 9th March. Support workers will start doing the school shifts on 1st March & nurses will stay at hospital ready for when we get back from school. Praying this will be an easy transition for everyone. Enjoyed a shopping trip with Samuel to select chests of drawers & a tv unit. Have a great week! XO

**05.03.17   Week 66      Day 462**

Samuel has had a good week, he's well and enjoying school. Support workers have started, don't like being in position to be their boss when in our company, but guess that will ensure they are doing things for Samuel the way we need them to. Our house is looking like it's close to being ready. Surgery on Wednesday is still going ahead. That's us for this week. Hope you have a great week. Blessings, XO

**12.03.17   Week 67      Day 469**

Week 67 less than 2 weeks in our hospital stay to go...discharge is coming! Samuel will have surgery again in 3 months for a repeat of Trache and lungs check. Lungs are looking good, trachea below tube is good, however granulation tissue was removed from above his Trache. About 80% of trachea was blocked by granulation. Not good. The body is amazing the way it tries to repair itself. Sadly though, this granulation tissue will keep growing, trying to heal, but if undetected it will grow too big, potentially causing a blockage. The good & the bad of our bodies. Exciting part of week was starting to move in to our house. A few finishing touches to come inside this week before Samuel comes home to stay. Wishing you a great week:) XO

**19.03.17   Week 68      Day 476**

Week 68 was a busy one with school, house sorting and unpacking, & finalising things with the hospital teams. Samuel participated in the school cross country race, his own circuit developed by him during the term. Have a 'See you later Samuel' party to attend on Tuesday late arvo, on lead up to discharge on Thursday! On day 480, the three of us will take our Samuel out of those PICU glass doors for hopefully at least 3 months. It will be with mixed emotions as we leave, so happy to be going home as a family, very relieved to be not driving up to a couple of hours extra each day, and finally a little sad to say goodbye to the amazing staff whom we have been greeted by, chatted with, laughed with, cried in presence of, and most importantly trusted  with Samuel's life for what will be 480  days. Huge week ahead, much love XO

**26.03.17   Week69   Day 480 discharge   Text on Day 483**

Woohoo, Samuel has done it...discharged on Day 480 as expected! We enjoyed a 'See ya later Sam' party on the balcony of PICU. Caught up with numerous personnel who have & also a number who haven't worked with Samuel. Highlight of evening would have to be Dexter the dog visiting. Hadn't seen him for about 3 months as Samuel was always out when he visited.

It was very emotional as Samuel drove around PICU on his way towards the big glass PICU doors where staff popped party poppers as he drove through. He then headed to level 2 where he was greeted by a guard of honour organised by the media/comms personnel at the request of the hospital CEO, to cheer him out. The media section put his exit on Children's Health Qld Lady Cilento Facebook page if you want to have a look. The transition to home has been pretty good. It will take a while training the support workers as they start working with Samuel, but we look forward to their next shifts where they are better informed and know Samuel better each time. Can you believe it, we are home to stay? How beautiful to be able to watch your child sleeping, and then go to bed! (without driving home first) Well, what will you do on Sunday nights now that our messages will stop? Relax, that's my Sunday night plan. Actually, we might let you know some updates as/when they happen in the future. Let us know if you've had enough, won't bother us at all. Please keep Samuel in your prayers that one day there might just be a break through to perhaps enhance his body's ability. We are never giving up hope! Thank you for being part of Samuel's journey and being there for our family. Look after yourselves & your family and enjoy life! Many blessings, Jane, Craig, Amelia and Samuel XOXO

www.ingramcontent.com/pod-product-compliance
Lightning Source LLC
Chambersburg PA
CBHW070348090426
42733CB00009B/1329